Retirement
How <u>Not</u> To End Up
Tired,
Bored
and
Lonely

Joel E. Smith

ISBN – 10:1717049060
ISBN-13:9781717049063

Front cover photo credit: www.stmichaelschurch.co.uk

DEDICATION

To Priscilla

"Life is a Banquet
and
Most Poor Bastards
are Starving"

Retirement: How Not To End Up Tired, Bored and Lonely

ABOUT THE AUTHOR

Joel has interviewed hundreds of retirees over 15 years to gain insight into a successful life. These interviews, along with sound scientific research, form the basis of the recommendations in this book.

Joel Smith was Clear Computing's co-founder, vice-president, and Chief Technology Officer. He was educated at the State University of New York at Stony Brook, receiving a B.S. in physics, and at John Carroll University, where he received an M.A.T. in physics education. Joel has been a business consultant and software designer for the waste management industry since 1988. He previously held positions as an industrial engineer, finance controller and system designer for Johns-Manville, American Cyanamid and Allied Chemical. At AT&T Bell Laboratories, Joel was a Distinguished Member of Technical Staff.

Joel is the author of <u>Fitting the Pieces Together: A Guide to Office Operations for the Liquid Waste Industry</u> and was a regular columnist in a number of service publications, including the Pumper, American Recycler, and Sanitation Journal. His articles on the impact of new technologies on the service industry focus on the practical issues of business benefits and implementation for small and medium-sized operations. Joel has also been a frequent speaker at Environmental Expo, and at regional waste conferences.

CONTENTS

ACKNOWLEDGMENTS

To all the men and women who have taken the time to share their feelings, concerns, and problems. Their openness will help all of us have a much happier second life.

To my family for understanding and cooperation in my journey to find a path to happiness, pleasure, and purpose.

To Dr. Kristi White who helped me understand the true purpose of exercise and how smart the human body is in adapting and changing.

Finally, to the many authors who helped me in the process of writing and their guidance in help me turn thoughts and emotions into words.

PREFACE

This book started 20 years ago in the lunchroom of Bell Laboratories in Holmdel New Jersey.

The labs closed several departments and had given early retirement to the department heads. Sitting in the lunch room, I saw several of these men who had their health, money, and family come back to work as contractors and have the same sandwich and cup of soup that had for their entire career. Given that they could do anything they wanted to. **Why did they return to work after having been retired?**

Department heads managed 50 to 500 plus highly skilled staff and had budgets in the millions. They were picked from the pool of the very best at Bell Laboratories. Bell Labs hired from around the world and rule of thumb is that they only brought in the top 5% of candidate pools to be considered. The department heads were smart, highly educated, community members, had prosperous families and financially independent by all measures and they still returned to work.

Over the years I met and interviewed men at the gym, on vacations, and in business, listening to the stories and choices they made about retirement. I continued this hobby. Then I sold a software company I had built and retired. I was out shopping with my wife and stopped at a traffic light not far from the company office and realized that I had had a lovely day and enjoyed lunch and was "comfortable." The next realization was that my head was empty. I was not thinking about the company, employees, technology, operations, support and the list goes on. All gone. **My purpose in life that involved most of my waking hours was gone. At that moment I knew why the department heads went back to work.**

I was lonely, bored and a little scared. I had followed all the rules of saving for retirement and having hobbies, yet I felt my life was over. I am well trained in many fields, most of which centered around solving difficult problems. This book came out of the journey of me finding a new life and purpose in retirement. Retirement is a difficult problem, and this book is intended to help solve it.

In any endeavor, it is important to maintain a focus on the value-added proposition. In business, if you try to be all things to all people, you generally fail. This book is written from the viewpoint of a principal wage earner.

INTRODUCTION

This book tells the story of denial, procrastination, uncertainty, and doubt that you go through as you approach and enter retirement. The viewpoint taken is that of the principal wage earner. The chapters focus on alternative paths that can be taken and **why the recommendation "all you need is money," is not true.** It is also a must-read for spouses of retirees to better understand the severe impact that retirement has on their partner.

A path is described to becoming healthier and stronger, while learning to see yourself and those around you in a different light, e.g., a paradigm shift. Things do not change, how you look at them changes. You are retired and have left the principal purpose of your life behind: your career to maintain the financial stability of your family, your "big money career." The book's approach is to make you aware of the alternatives and help you see them clearly, so you can feel good about your choices. You are guided using physical fitness routines, a change in eating habits with a set of aids to minimize boredom and improve your awareness of who you are, so you can choose your path in retirement. These are the last years of your life. You have worked hard, supported your family and saved and have an expectation that you will enjoy and prosper during retirement. **A fair expectation, but unfortunately, not a guarantee.**

You are faced with retirement, the real thing, not an urban legend or a marketing blurb from the so-many financial houses on how they can help you live to be 200 years old while you play polo. Until now, you had gotten up every day and gone to work, even when people waiting for you at work wanted to make your life hard, you went to work. Snow, rain, cold and gas shortages, you went to work. Take a moment to appreciate the sense of purpose, accomplishment, passion, and fulfillment that it gave you. **Now it is gone!**

Talk about going from an active social and productive environment to isolation and boredom![i] Unfortunately, this is not the only challenge you are facing. Your career is gone, but most likely, so is your body. Commuting daily to work, sitting at a desk, and time itself have added pounds and weakened muscles. These, along with hearing loss and vision changes all affect your ability to succeed in retirement. You are facing a new challenge which will require your body to be there to support you. The book guides you through activities that strengthen your body, entertains you and creates an opportunity for you to see who you are now. We recommend the tools that alleviate the boredom and create the opportunities for feelings of accomplishment so that you can build upon your successes.

Here are some simple tests to see how fit you are. You will see that mobility is key to several of the alternatives. There are three parts to this test. The tests are not pass/fail; they are more to make you aware of your body. You need to see yourself for who and what you are. No judgment or evaluation, just clear vision. The purpose is to help you look at your body and your fitness condition so you can guide your choices going forward.

First, can you get up from a straight back chair without using your upper body to stand up? Yes, you have spent the last 30 plus years getting into the car, sitting at a desk and pushing a pencil. Now stand up. Not so easy?

Second, try putting your pants on without sitting or leaning against a wall. Huh, a real challenge?

The third and final test is to walk up a flight of stairs without using the railing. We suggest placing the back of your hand against the rail to steady yourself, so you do not fall down the stairs.

If you found the test a challenge, it should guide your choices. We have two sections that cover in detail a stepping program and an eating regime to help you transition to a fitness level so that you can move forward:

- Fitness – A Method of Self Awareness
- Fitness – Eating Program

The chapters on fitness are designed to keep you entertained with activities that can help you find your body and give you a sense of accomplishment and fun, rather than the pain and suffering associated with fitness programs centered around raising heart rates, stress training, and calorie restriction. You must remember you are not 20 years old. You may look beautiful on the outside, but the truth is, as you age, your tendons, muscles, and bones have weakened with time. When they are stressed, they break. Think of your body like a shiny white plastic chair, clean upright with no cracks, but has been outside in the weather for years. When stressed, the chair, like your body, will shatter. You end up recovering for months in pain. Retirement means you will be using your body in different ways than the last 30 years. We like to say that we help you find your body so you can use it going forward.

The eating regime is designed around helping you see yourself and be free of the addictive drug-like effects of sugar and carbohydrates. These are quick energy and comfort foods you have depended upon for your physical and mental ability at work. The results of these foods are drug-like. They are addictive and cause anxiety and energy peaks and valleys. The addiction is the same as the cigarette industry saying smoking is a matter of free will, even though they knew the addictive effects of tobacco. The modern diet of processed and high carbohydrate meals is not free will; it is a chemical addiction that results in you being out of shape, overweight and stressed. The chapter on "Fitness – Eating Regine" guides you away from foods that stimulate your hunger and raise your anxiety. The program recommended is based on science and allows you to enjoy eating and feel at one with your body.

Seeing your body and becoming free of the drug-like effects of sugars and carbs is the just the beginning. The other changes are as significant as those you went through during puberty. You ask, "Since puberty?" Bigger and more challenging than sex drive, dating, picking a hairstyle, figuring out how to sign your name and how to dress?" **Yes, it is a new beginning.**

Let me share with you some of the many surprises that retirement has in store for you. Let's start with your partner in life. Do you know that divorce rates for those over 55 are up 110% and it is the wife who mostly initiates them?[ii] Yes, your partner in life may want you to leave? You say, "my wife will never divorce me." Well, guess what? For the last 30 years, you typically started early, came home late and many times worked weekends. Your sharing centered on the house, career, children, and acquisition of stuff. Now, suddenly, you are 24x7 with your partner and most of the activities you have built your life around are gone.

We will tell you a story of Jim, his wife and a butcher's knife that will help you feel what is happening when you try to stay home.[iii] The book enables you to see the paradigm shift you will need to experience to have a successful marriage in retirement. It shows you that this is a time of re-establishing your relationship with your wife in a manner very similar to when you first met.

Let's see how your work friends respond to this new you. You're sociable and have a full contact list of people you have worked with for many years, sharing your life. You reach out and *slam,* the door never opens. A quick example so you can begin to feel how drastic a change is occurring. Alex was a director of a large company's maintenance division. He had thousands of people that worked for him and hundreds of peers. He stayed on past retirement age until 70 because he believed he was irreplaceable. Finally, at 70 he retired to be with his wife, who was fighting cancer. This man deferred his retirement for five years and during that time had to deal with the medical challenges of a critically sick wife. He went back the following summer to say hello to his longtime friends and could not even get into the building. **I remind you that at work, you are all paid to be friends**.

So, your work is gone, your friends have full-time activities, and you will discover that your wife has built a full life with you as only a part-time player, and your children are on their own journeys. So, you refocus on fixing up the house. With nothing to distract you, you can see all the projects not finished and the "wish I had time to do" projects. These projects, along with golfing buddies and vacations, may buy you 12 to 18 months and then you're back to waking early and possibly going to the gym looking to strike up a conversation or end up sitting watching TV news for the company. It sounds harsh because it is. **As we said, it's as tough as growing up, if not harder.**

The key to a successful journey is that you need to feel and see your new world so that you can guide yourself. This seeing yourself and the people around you is called "a paradigm shift." While you worked your "big money career," people knew how to relate to you. You were the bread-winner, boss, wage-earning husband, etc. and now it is different; you are no longer any of these. You are retired.

Your life has been the achievement of a series of milestones like getting a job, building a family, owning a home and having children. Being successful in your career is a well-worn path that is fully funded and staffed to take new people in and move them along their career path, rewarding them as they go. Retirement is not that way. When you retire, none of the training and motivational aids you have depended upon apply. You are on your own.

In this book, we guide you through this new territory and help you in "seeing and feeling" the new milestones of a successful retirement. The keys to these milestones are not what, but how, when and with whom.

We use some phases throughout the book that have a specific interpretation. Here is a list of terms with descriptions. Each of these is further described and built upon within the individual chapters.

- **Big Money Career** – The career you followed to earn money to support your family.
- **Nuclear family** - Your spouse and children.
- **Tribal** – The non-nuclear family, friends, and neighbors. There are several tribes, a different one for each member of your family.
- **Acquaintance** - People you know by name and share a common purpose, e.g., work, neighbor
- **Friend** – This is a special person in your life. You typically can call them for help and they come, you trust them and share your personal feelings. Almost like a family member. Last but not least, you have broken bread and shared each other's company.
- **Purpose** – The emotions and feelings you have surrounding your "big money career."
- **Grandparent Dom** – When you spend your waking hours helping your wife care for the grandchildren.
- **Waiting** – When you spend your retirement taking no active action to expand your life.
- **Paradigm Shift** – When how you see the world around you changes, rather than the things around you changing.
- **Gym Junkie** – Spends long hours at the gym making small talk with acquaintances who never become friends.

Leaning to deal with the reality of retirement is not a silver-bullet (quick and easy answer), or straightforward process. We help you to see and experience the paradigm shifts needed to be successful in retirement and for you to understand all the opportunities around you.

You will be facing several alternatives, each of which is valid, and a path that you might follow. It is not a question of one being better than the other. You have worked hard and followed all the rules. The book helps guide you through the choices, so you are not Lonely, Tired and Bored. The categories of retirement lifestyles that the book expands on are:

1. Daily activities grow to fill the time
2. Continue to work
3. Grandparent Dom
4. Waiting
5. Paradigm Shift - so you can see yourself for who you are, your passions and activities that can be developed to give you a purposeful retirement

In the following chapters, we develop a method for you to find and build your purpose so that you can spend your retirement years involved with a sense of personal accomplishment.

RETIREMENT – THE MARKETING FANTASY

The Truth of What Happens When You Retire

The truth about retirement is that you lose all your connections, your wife wants you out of the house, you may be too old to work, and many of the volunteer options are limited to activities that only require a warm body, boiled down to the simplest of tasks. An older body physically challenges you, and the trainers and gyms have programs for the "younger, stronger and faster generation." They have you doing things for 20 and 30-year-olds which your 60+-year-old body shouldn't do.

You may end up sitting at the local coffee shop with a laptop doing nothing, or the gym looking for someone to make small talk. Once the morning is over, you get to go home and watch the news. You have all this money, time and experience and a busy day means you get to go to the post office.

Expectations - The Setup

You may expect retirement to be the same as all the other milestones you accomplished. Let's look at a typical journey. You start young, healthy and have the world in front of you. The road ahead is well lit and marked. If you wander off, a bunch of people and institutions remind you about getting back on the path to success. You are a success and become an adult when you achieve the milestones of career, marriage, own a home and have children. It feels right, and there is so much stuff to do, people to play with and many exciting challenges to take. Let's bring back the memories to appreciate what a great time you had.

In high school, your family spent the time and resources to give you experience and opportunities at building your body (sports), your mind, social skills (scouts, religious training, camps) and learning leadership and responsibility. They were with you every step of the way. You were never alone, with parents and family there to guide and help at any indication of need.

College was a time with friends, a safe place to live, and lots of food. Daily challenges and great learning experiences that were interesting and stimulating to you were everywhere. You got to try learning different things, and if you did not like it, you merely changed your major, and you were off to a new group of guides (teachers) and tribe members (other students) with similar interests. You even had respected leaders (faculty advisors) work with you in the rituals and challenges to enhance your experience and increase your successes. Let's not forget the social whirlwind of concerts, teams, guest speaker events, and all those people working full time to include you.

It seemed that everyone around you, tribe members, teachers, and family spent every moment trying to link you up and get you involved with school, career, and partners in life. Each choice you made had rewards and praise. Internships allowed you to play at being employed without the downsides. Backpack vacations let you see and experience mini-quests. Then came the planning, so many decisions on clothing, food and much of it brand new to your life.

Let us not forget the relationships, the sharing and bonding of so many firsts. Every step brought a wonderful feeling of accomplishment and growth. The glow of stepping forward towards being an adult. The accomplishment of the critical milestones of adulthood, relationships.

Let's move forward to graduation, more presents, and a brand-new tribe, a company, respected elders to give guidance (supervisors and executives) and so many new people to play with (co-workers and customers). You got to grow and adapt to new challenges as an individual and tribal member (employee of the company). Also, you added a newly expanded community to your life, your nuclear family.

Yes, a family. A spouse and a place to live with so many great things to buy and create your beautiful, comfortable space. That first one-bedroom apartment. The intimacy and every minute the bonding of two souls. You were tied at the hip, and both worked at sharing, and acceptance of differences and compromises.

You were now experiencing the full support, counseling, and companionship that society, your employment, the extended and nuclear family could offer. In every direction, there were people and organizations to help, guide and correct your choices, so you were successful. Indeed, that was a honeymoon period that was unmatched so far in your life. Let us pause and review how tremendous and complete were the support, physical ability, and experiences that surrounded you. Let's see, you had all the following:

You were physically at your best
New clothing
Excitement of career
On Job Training at work
Supervisors grooming you for growth
Co-workers all sharing the same journey
Projects to test your skills and build experience
Your extended family for help and advice on where to live
When should you start a family?
How to save for retirement?
Offering help with buying a home
Invitations to family get-togethers for you to share your new nuclear family
Partner with whom you are one
Partner to build a comfortable living space
Partner that is there to listen, discuss and work alternatives to all of life's issues
Spending me-centered vacations
… And much more

Everything was at its best. You had challenges that supported a future that you could be impassioned about and made you **feel a *real purpose*, to provide for your family.**

Just to let you know how powerful and meaningful this purpose is for men, when you ask men who are facing death what single thing they need to accomplish so they can pass in peace, it was to "provide for my family."[iv]

Through your life's journey, you expected that this vast array of services and support would be there for you. All you must do is earn money, to provide for your family.

Journey to the Reality - It's Not Only You!

We now come to one of the significant paradigm shifts you went through as part of your journey to success, having children. Up to now, you had a vast array of support and comradery. You had money, career, a beautiful home, and a partner who is at one with you. You were guided to the next milestone by your extended family and wife who was feeling the need to have a baby. What a great idea, all that fooling around, new places to shop and lots of good stuff to do, e.g., prepare the nursery, discuss names, baby showers. You felt great you were going to be a dad.

Your partner was focused on you and your needs. She may have had an outside job, but when you were together, it was all about you, your career and the nuclear family. When you watched a sporting event, you were together. She was there with you. **That was about to change is a big way.**

This partner, your one and only, was about to find another. Your baby was born, and after a few months you were back at work, and your wife was now a mother. Your partner who you ate with, went to the movies, fooled around all over the house and had such good times, was now partnered up with another. Let's see how women answered the same question men where asked about what the one thing is they need to accomplish before they pass. Women responded that it would be to look at their children through life's milestones, christening, graduations, etc., and if the women did not have children, they mentioned nieces and nephews. Notice they did not say "husbands", you are essential, but not on the list to answer the question if they can pass in peace.

Here's a little story so you can feel the intensity of that relationship.

Imagine that you and your family are walking down a street and your child runs into the street and is about to be hit, fatally by a car. The only way to save your child is to throw yourself in front of the vehicle, almost certain death. Do you hesitate, no? You must protect your child. Now, the same situation, but it is your wife who is about to be hit by the car. Did you feel the difference? That bond between parent and child is exceptional. It is the one thing a woman says must be completed to die in peace.

So, you understand the degree of change that was about to happen: You were going to lose the individual attention of your life's partner's support and be asked to support your wife in her journey through motherhood. A significant turnaround, loss, and now you had to do the heavy lifting. The story of the impact of children to a nuclear family is several books by itself. The message here is that this beautiful life and this blessed event with all its wonder, expectations and future promises, came with unexpected significant changes and responsibilities where you were not the center.

But you then had an expanded nuclear family. A tribe that brought in so many great things like joining the Indian Princesses, Scouts, playgroups, religious training, possibly a new home with better schools and your career was expanding. Things were changing all around you that emphasized your primary life goal of supporting your family. But you still felt the change with your partner.

Your wife had started her life's purpose, and it challenged all her abilities. Even her mom came to help with the transition, but that time passed, and she became a mother. A mother first and, most importantly, a wife second. During this time of change, to be successful, you went through a paradigm shift. You saw yourself and relationships with those around you differently. For you, this took place over an extended period, planning for children, trying to get pregnant, pregnancy, and the first year of your first child's life. It took a lot of time, people, and effort.

Your efforts focused on providing for your family and supporting your wife, with the guidance of the nuclear and tribal family. You were at work, building your career. You wife was creating and maintaining the family. Together, yet separate.

You were both busy. You might have felt some isolation and separateness, but your career more than filled the void. You were the "big money" provider. Even so, can you now feel the paradigm shift from husband to father and from a couple to a family? In this shift, everyone you touched supported your change. Retirement, in contrast, is entirely different. **In retirement, you are on your own.**

Alternative Paths in Retirement

The transition to retirement is typically, "do not let the door hit you on the way out." You are working and doing some shifting of responsibilities if needed, and then you are not at work any longer. You have centered your life on providing for your family and supporting and growing your career. Yes, that thing that filled your head 24x7.

You were working, and now you are not. You had a whole tribe of work relationships; now you do not. You reach out to tribal and nuclear family, and they have built their own lives over the last 30 years of your career building. The tribal members are not employees that follow strict guidelines and relationships, like on the job. They do not know you as a 24x7 live-in. They know so little about you, that when you sit down to discuss what to do they say:

- What hobbies do you have?
- Go for a walk
- Call a friend and go fishing.
- Play golf

All these things are breaks from working; they are not full-time activities that supply purpose in your life.

Your purpose in life just ended. The money is needed, but you are redundant. Your wife has her career that does not include you sitting at home meddling in her world she has been responsible for and managing for 30 years. Let me tell you a little story about Jim's experience.

Jim was a trainer at a large telecommunication company. He had a medical condition, so he received early retirement at close to full pay. His in-laws passed away and left him real estate holdings worth millions that Jim sold tax-free. To top that, he had property near a mall that needed to expand, and he was able to sell it for a tidy sum. You might say he had all the money he would ever need, and early retirement, so he was set up for the rest of his life. A dream come true.

He used his honeymoon period of retirement and his wife's willingness and purchased a Winnebago to see the country. He took his wife away from her tribe, extended family, and his children. She went with him, but soon the Winnebago had its side destroyed pulling into a gas station, and they were back home. Jim then looked for work and only found a series of retail sales jobs, and he ended up selling appliances at Sears to fill his days. He gave that up and stayed home. After several weeks his wife sat with him at the kitchen table and said she had something important to tell him. She then placed a butcher's knife between them, his loving and caring wife, and explained that if he was not out of the (her) house at 9:00 am every day, she said lovingly, that she would take this butchers knife to his body.

Jim called me asking for some computer help. He had rented a one-person office in the local downtown, purchased some state-of-the-art computers and hung up a shingle "Computer Training." Jim found himself a beautiful office with two windows in a building filled with small offices. He went to that office every day and socialized with other business in the office. Out at 9:00 and back by 5:00. He just could not see a new image of himself in retirement, a paradigm shift. **So, he went back to make-believe work.**

Oh, you think, this is an exception. Sadly, this is not the case. How about the business entrepreneur who retired at 61 who walks 3-5 miles every morning, then goes to the gym hot tub and track until he can go home to have lunch with his wife or play golf. Then there was the broker who made it big and bragged about taking a helicopter to the top of a 9000-foot mountain to ski down and told his financial advisor that he considered it a busy day when he went to the post office. These people had expectations of support and tribal involvement in their retirement, like at every other milestone in their lives.

This great awakening is that you are suitable for some short-term conspicuous consumption (bucket lists) and then need to stay out of the way of everyone else who is earning a living or growing a family. They will let you volunteer for some simple tasks like serving food, setting up tables. Jobs with "Purpose" are another thing. Activities with a purpose come with a salary to make sure you show up regularly; they are called jobs.

To have a successful retirement, you need to see yourself, everyone else and things around you not through the eyes that you have trained for the last 30 years, but a new view, "a paradigm shift" that will support you seeing and finding your revised purpose.

What is a paradigm shift? It's a change in how you view the world around you. Let me share with you a story from the book Seven Habits Of Highly Effective People by Stephen Covey.[v]

"I remember a mini-Paradigm Shift I experienced one Sunday morning on a subway in New York.
People were sitting quietly -- some reading newspapers; some lost in thought, some resting with their eyes closed. It was a calm, peaceful scene.

Then suddenly, a man and his children entered the subway car. The children were so loud and rambunctious that instantly the whole climate changed.

The man sat down next to me and closed his eyes, apparently oblivious to the situation. The children were yelling back and forth, throwing things, even grabbing people's papers. It was very disturbing. And yet, the man sitting next to me did nothing.

It was difficult not to feel irritated. I could not believe that he could be so insensitive to let his children run wild like that and do nothing about it, taking no responsibility at all. It was easy to see that everyone else on the subway felt irritated, too. So finally, with what I felt was unusual patience and restraint, I turned to him and said, "Sir, your children are really disturbing a lot of people. I wonder if you couldn't control them a little more?"

The man lifted his gaze as if to come to a consciousness of the situation for the first time and said softly, "Oh, you're right. I guess I should do something about it. We just came from the hospital where their mother died about an hour ago. I don't know what to think, and I guess they don't know how to handle it either."

Can you imagine what I felt at that moment? My paradigm shifted. Suddenly I saw things. Differently, I felt. Differently, I behaved differently. My irritation vanished. I didn't have to worry about controlling my attitude or my behavior; my heart was filled with the man's pain. Feelings of sympathy and compassion flowed freely. 'Your wife just died? Oh, I'm so sorry. Can you tell me about it? What can I do to help?" Everything changed in an instant.

Many people experience a similar fundamental shift in thinking when they face a life-threatening crisis and suddenly see their priorities in a different light, or when they suddenly step into a new role, such as that of husband or wife, parent or grandparent, manager or leader."

Paths Available

In retirement, several paths are available for selection. You can:

1. Create busy tasks to fill the time.
2. Go back to work.
3. Join Grandparent Dom.
4. Sit around waiting.
5. A paradigm shift to find the things that give you pleasure, happiness, and purpose.

Let's briefly look at each these alternatives in what a typical day and week consist of so you can see the options to guide your choice. Each is just a choice, equal, for you to consider. The idea is not to be surprised, but to be aware of the real possibilities. You have now realized that your primary purpose in life is over, yes, over. That purpose to provide for the family was successful, and now you are redundant.

Make Tasks Fill the Time

Typically, the first path people attempt after retiring. You are home and get up at the same time you always did. If your wife is still sleeping, so you go and turn on the TV to a news channel for the company. Make yourself a cup of coffee and wait. You start looking around your home, which, by the way, your wife has managed for the last thirty years, and you begin to think about the home repairs and projects. You are using the skills you used on the job to succeed. The only problem is, this is your wife's domain. You team up with her and get your space cleaned up and organized doing what you did part time, only now it is full time. Doing these will buy you a year at best and then you are right back to "emptiness."

Your wife has her life, tribes, and activities and they do not include you. She has been building that over the last 30 years meeting her purpose in life which is to see the children through their life milestones. You have been at work. So, you reach out to golfing buddies, and you can find some for the weekend, but they are working. Soon it becomes clear you need something to do, maybe a hobby in the basement, or woodworking in the garage by yourself. If that starts to sound like a minimum-security prison with kitchen privileges, it is. Living without a tribe is very, very lonely. Let me give you an example of the way your day could play out to try to fill the time.

If you go to any YMCA with a pool, you will most likely find a "master's swim group." The group is made up of swimmers trying to capture the comradery and purpose of being on a swim team. They are up at 5 am to get pool time, and to make timed sprints. Trouble is you are not 17 years old, and your body does not have the endurance or strength, and so you are either back to watching cable news or hanging out at the gym making conversation, killing time until you can head home for lunch.

Another example is you go out walking and then head to the gym for a shower and some machine time until lunch. You may be able to volunteer one day a week in the afternoon in some charity effort. You are trying to fill a 10 to 12-hour day, five days a week, that was your career and guess what; there is nothing to do that gives you a sense of fulfillment. Almost all the volunteer work has been boiled down to tasks that anyone walking in the door can do.

What you find yourself doing is slowing down and making the activity expand to fit the free time. That morning cup of coffee now runs until 11 am. Lunch takes two hours. You go to the coffee shop and sit all morning long, looking at the same news sites to see if anything changed. The typical description people use is "I do not know how I got things done when I was working. I am busy all day."

An alternative way to live out your second life may be hobbies in the basement and garage, watching T.V., accompanying your wife to lunch three times a week, after spending five hours in the gym making small talk with gym junkies.

Work

Continuing to work is a solution for some when facing retirement. They are asked to stay on because they are invaluable and do such a great job. The sad truth is either the organization does not want to do the heavy lifting to find and train a replacement, or the cost to replace you would be more than they are paying you now. Bottom line, no one in a business is irreplaceable. Your work is your perceived tribe, people who you socialize with and may call friends. Unfortunately, they are not friends, they are work acquaintances. A little story to help you feel the difference between a friend and an acquaintance.

Jill worked in a leading technical organization and headed the lab that supported a four-year effort to prepare a state of the art system for the Olympics. She had over 100 of the best minds working directly with her, and they represented thousands of people in development, manufacturing and quality assurance, a significant intense effort. The job was done and done right. One day she complained of pain in her back, two weeks later she passed away from cancer. Here it comes. Once news spread that she had passed, security had to be called to lock her office because people where scavenging her possessions from the office before her family could come in. Wait, the lack of real friendship gets worse. When a notice went out to her funeral, not one of the hundred professionals who worked closely with her for four years showed up. **You are paid to be friendly acquaintances at work, not friends.**

Staying at work is easier than the emptiness and challenge of building your second life. At least there is a tribe and a continuation of purpose if you stay at work. If you leave, "Do not let the door hit you on the way out." was a comment to a lead contributor on their last day at the job. The door has already shut, so you look for work, and you get "overqualified" which is another way of saying you are too old. So, you take a retail job. One man took a job a McDonalds at the counter. Tough work for an old body, the good news is he ate a French fry from a customer's tray and was fired.

Remember the golden field of jobs and excitement when you started out. You will not find the support and alternatives that you saw when you were part of the workforce. You will work part-time. Here is a story to help you see the workplace, in a kind of "paradigm shift." Jake was head of a maintenance department in an extensive organization. He retired late and took a three day a week job at a local nursery selling plants and maintaining the displays. Plants were his passion, and Jake saw this as an opportunity to be involved and share his extensive knowledge and skill. He did a great job and did it well. After a few months, his boss called him in and wanted to promote him to a full-time position to the supervisor of other hourly workers handling the plants. Jake respectfully declined the full-time job, he only wanted a three day a week job. He was asked to leave; his position is part of the career growth for other employees.

Work to meet your purpose of providing for your family is not a true tribe. Hopefully, you are starting to "see" that "gainful employment" is just an activity to provide for your family. You were part of the mainstream of business before retirement. After you retired, you are no longer in the main business flow. If you go back to work to fill the time, you are marginal and, most likely, so is the type of work that you are doing.

Still, continuing to work is in the spirit of using life's essential tools, "procrastination" and "denial." You may stay at work until the inevitable medical event of aging impacts your abilities and makes work impossible; then you choose one of the other alternatives to living out your life. Sounds harsh but seeing your "real life" so you can make informed choices is not easy.

Grandparent Dom

A special case is when your children defer marriage and children, and you have multiple grandchildren that live within fifteen minutes of your home. By the way, if you are not within 15 minutes, you will be moving. You become childcare for your grandchildren. Your wife is now grandchild-centric, and you are the "go for" for your wife and son or daughter and playmate for your grandchildren.

You follow your wife, and she guides you through your responsibilities. Your pulse changes over to "baby time," sitting and holding the baby and hours go by in a blink. You can nap on the couch, and your grandchildren will sleep on your chest or cover you and snuggle. Real unconditional love, acceptance, and purpose all rolled up into a nuclear and tribal family.

Supporting your grandchildren carries you through the initial decade of uncertainty and boredom. You do not even have to go to the gym.

Waiting

Waiting was expressed to me by an 86-year-old as "waiting for dirt." Sounds terrible, and it is an alternative that some use because the effort to see and live a new life is just too intense. I mean it. Think back to what it took to accomplish your milestones in your career. The time, effort, angst and living with the uncertainty took all you had and then some. You also had a partner, and both of you knew for sure what you were doing. Your primary purpose was to build and provide for your family.

Well, guess what, you have, and it's over. You must start over again only this time all the guideposts, trainers, support and rewards typically just do not exist. Physically you are not at your best and lack the strength. When active, you quickly tire, and your body has worn down and does not have the flexibility and bounce of your younger years. You have the perfect cover; I am old, I do not have money, I am not physically fit and on and on and on. You can make your favorite past time visiting the doctor's office. All those tests, each taking a day or more and so many specialists, so many appointments, almost a full-time job.

With time you become less fit. You love to chain-watch old movies. You take frequent naps; you do not have the energy. Even regular shopping becomes a challenge. You visit family less; trips to have fun become more and more limited, because of the weather, it's harder to walk, and the expense is too high. It doesn't matter why, it only matters that you are not engaged. You are waiting for the next thing to happen to you, which is not you are interacting with your life.

You are waiting for life to come to you. If it only worked that way. Your family may make the time to reach out and "bring you along." So, you have a favorite chair, favorite TV programs, or a book club that meets once a month. You continue until the inevitable medical issues of body and soul not being used, and father time is bringing you closer and closer to your unavoidable incapacitation and/or death.

What are the "tells" that can indicate you are waiting? Well, the well-worn clothing, the worn-out favorite chair you refuse to change out even with the help of family, and the diminishing circle of friends. You like to sit quietly at home and catch up. Real aging comes to all of us. Hands shake, memory fades, and the strength to move our body diminishes. To some, sooner than others, but we all go there before we pass. For some, this is the best and, possibly, only path. The individual chooses this journey and easily justifies the choice at the time. We hope to raise your awareness of the alternatives so you can make a conscious decision on the alternative path you want to follow.

Paradigm Shift for Purposes of Life

This alternative sounds different because it is. To begin with, you cannot buy it at Walmart, Target or Amazon. Sadly, your wife and extended nuclear family cannot help you, even though it makes it easier to find them at fault as the cause of your retirement woes. You are also not at fault, but you are the root of the solution.

This journey will take your full attention. It includes physical fitness, proper eating regime, and openness to who you are, and the many choices made over your lifetime. You have made hundreds, if not thousands, of decisions that have made up your life. Some of these were done at a very young age but have stayed with you, like a duckling following the first image it sees when coming out of the egg. These choices could be part of your memory, these choices are the fabric that is you.

In the following chapters, we will go over paradigm shifts on exercise, eating regimes, your home, vacation activities and, yes, your nuclear family, to help you experience as many changes in views as possible. By now, you know I live to tell little stories to bring a point across. These two stories talk about the inside of your "soul" where there are alternative lives that you may have suppressed or left behind to meet your purpose.

A successful business banker who worked on Wall Street and commuted to a NJ suburb took early retirement, made peace with his wife of thirty years and two sons and came out as gay. He then moved to live in an apartment in a gay community. His sons and wife understood and supported this change in his life to make his inner self-complete. He met his primary purpose, and then and only then did the transition to his new life. An amazing story of commitment and caring for his nuclear family.

Then there was the medical professional who retired and opened a one-person handyman business. He loved working with his hands and interacting with homeowners and their neighbors. He spent time doing small jobs in a limited neighborhood where everyone knew him and his work. A far cry from the stress and responsibilities of his career.

How can you see the alternatives that will give you inner peace, participation with an extended tribe and a full purpose in your daily life? You need to be able to find and see who you are. That person you built choice by choice from early childhood, through puberty and as an adult. You have spent almost your entire adult life creating and living this purpose. You need to find your "purpose" and peel back all the things you took on as supposed-to and looking-good that are now your daily life. Look for things that challenge you or you wanted to do but did not allow yourself.

Here is a task to start you on your journey of becoming aware of your choices and interacting with people around you. You need to choose a safe topic that almost everyone has an opinion on, and their view is ok no matter what it is. In the past, you have used your first purpose to justify your choices. Some that you may be familiar with are "Save first, spend second," "The children come first," "You need to finish what you start." **The objective is for you to honestly see another view as real and valid that is different than one you hold.**

Select a safe issue that you feel comfortable with and really believe your view is correct. Pick something that is judgmental like, "Artists are not really earning a living.", "It is not safe to talk with strangers." Or "Who makes the best ice cream?". You have made choices in your life that support these "beliefs." These were done to support your purpose of your big money career and support your family.

You will have to step outside your comfort zone. If you believe talking to strangers is wrong, talk to a good salesperson and get their view on what it is like speaking to strangers. Reach out to those around you and who believe differently. Work at seeing their view, not yours. The point is to see their view as valid even if different than yours. Talk to those around you about which manufacturer of ice cream they like best. Make an effort, buy several brands and try them to find the one you enjoy the most. It may take a little time to think about the differences and how they make you feel. Buy small containers, so you do not overeat. Be sensitive to the differences, and if they make you feel different. Make a list, you should talk to others, and the list will help. Think about ice cream as food, treat or a drug! Is ice cream a drug? What effect does it have on you? Do you eat it to satisfy hunger or another emotion? Is it a food that satisfies hunger or a mind-altering drug? How can ice cream be bad for you? Step back and open your beliefs to another view.

The purpose is to change how you view ice cream by engaging with others in exploring the different brands and versions of a flavor. Which plain old vanilla is best? Think about your relationship with these people you have engaged with discussing ice cream. Are these people very close to you? Are they part of a larger group who you socialize with, e.g., acquaintances, friends, neighbors? Have an ice cream tasting party, reach out to those around you and engage in conversation on brand, etc. Invite them to your home or a local restaurant. It will take some time and effort, and it is just you are changing your view on a favorite brand of ice cream, it is not your second life's purpose. Are you starting to see the role of ice cream differently? It is a thing you can safely share with others and establish a sharing group, or tribe. This change in how you see this food and its relation to you and your extended community is a paradigm shift. It is not just ice cream; it is the reason you are using to network and interact with those around you. Almost like a purpose of going to work and earn money, only this time it is linking in with a tribe (friends) and finding pleasure, happiness, and purpose, not just earning money.

Ice cream is a low impact effort. You can take on some other areas that will bring you out of your comfort zone. In every case, you need to reach out and be with people. These are just reasons to network; the objective is to network and to make friends to share with. Pick one that means something to you, so you are motivated:

- Afraid to fly. Take several short shuttle flights with a friend.

- Cannot swim. Learn to swim or take swimming lessons if you swim poorly.
- Afraid of heights, find the highest lookout points and join a group sightseeing.
- Pets are a waste of time and money. Get a pet, parakeets are a great start. Go to a class on parakeet training, any pet store will have some recommendations.
- Embarrassed to talk with strangers. Dress casual and ask to join a table at a mall eating area and introduce yourself. Tell them that you are practicing talking with strangers. Too stressful, get a haircut and talk with the barber. Go to a pharmacy and ask about alternative products for a skin rash.
- Cannot ride a bike. Join a bike club.

In retirement, your career and its tribe of co-workers no longer exist. If you do not want to sit home with the TV or buy a pet to have company, you will have to network. Remember those organization skills you had at work, go to it.

Now What?

Did you see yourself in any of the alternative paths?

1. Create busy tasks to fill the time.
2. Go back to work
3. Join Grandparent Dom
4. Sit around waiting
5. A paradigm shift. Find the things that give you pleasure, happiness, and purpose.

How did they make you feel? If you retire at 65, you can have 15 good years before your body and mind start to give way to aging. Aging means you begin to have less energy, sleep often and remember less. So how do you want to spend this time? Filling the time, engaging activities that give you pleasure, happiness, and purpose, or waiting?

The next chapters will take you through significant life components to help you start to see them not from the standpoint of the primary wage earner, but a person who is seeking to find him or herself in a new land. Later, we will help you in finding and empowering your body. We take you on the journey to see the body that is needed to support your new activities and purpose. At the same time, we give you some tools to reflect on your chosen self to see which path you want to pick to provide you with purpose, happiness, and fulfillment in this phase of your life. Think of fitness activities as a time for both physical and emotional training.

HOME - ANCHOR OR SAIL

Overview

You have lived in your home many decades. You raised a family, have a house filled with memories and souvenirs of your life passages. The home is joint ownership with every member of your family. You have over the many decades cooperated with your wife to fix, improve and expand your home. These were significant efforts with a visible benefit that was appreciated by all. You both know how to do this type of work and have good memories.

Now you are available 24x7 and can start to address the unfinished projects around the home. The starting point is the renovation and repair that have been put off. That new kitchen is now 25 years old. You could not afford the marble tops for the bathroom before, but you can now. You and your wife will team up as in the past and enjoy the bonding and joint effort of updating the home. This period where you do the things that gave you pleasure, a sense of accomplishment and sharing we call the "Honeymoon Period."

The "Honeymoon Period" can last 12 to 24 months and it includes home repair and enhancement, and vacations that were never taken, keeping you both occupied doing the things you have done together in the past. These were part of your joint effort in building and maintaining your family. You both know how to do these, have well-defined responsibilities, and it makes you feel good to have the work items out of the way and missed vacations taken.

Warning, warning. Being home fourteen hours a day you may start to think that things need to be changed, re-arranged, organized. I remind you that your home is your wife's. She has been living in it and responsible for it over the last 30+ years while you were at work. You may be on the title, but it is her career.

While you were living your big money career, your wife was building a nuclear family and extended tribe to keep your family whole. The home and the tribe are very tightly integrated. Your wife has been working very hard managing the separate little worlds that makeup suburbia. Let me share a short story about how much effort and stress your wife has gone through to build the tribe and keep the family whole.

Sally and Vick moved to a beautiful home off a county road. Vick worked at building his business and Sally was home with her firstborn. College-educated with extended family not local, she was alone with a newborn trying to make a home and deal with the stress of the first new baby. All by herself, she would go for walks around the neighborhood. Take a moment to feel the emotions, isolation, and the weight of the responsibility of a baby that your wife was dealing with, she was responsible for your child. One day a car screeched to a stop and a woman, Harriet, jumped out of the car and asked, "Do you live in this neighborhood?" They set up a play date and sat together in the living room with both babies on a blanket slobbering over the same toys. Sally asked Harriet if she was concerned about the germs, and she said "No." At that point, they were tribal members for life.

The intensity of these tribal relationships is compelling. Selling a home and moving away from these bonds is not easy or straightforward. These relationships are integral to everything your wife has been doing for the last 30 + years. A significant portion of your net worth may be in your home, but its location, content, and closeness to your wife's tribal contacts are a big part of who your wife and extended family are today. [vi]

You are still in business mode and may see the home as a physical and financial liability. The house you purchased for 100K$ is now worth 600K$, and the tax load has also grown to match. Putting money aside, you must heat, air condition, clean and repair the house, and you also face the grounds that need constant attention for all the seasons. Owning a home takes two people working together with resources just to keep it afloat. It is a cornerstone of your nuclear and extended tribe. You have been at work with a work centered tribe all who are paid to work and play well together, so they all make money. **Now, you are not at work.**

You are now living in your wife's world. You may see the house as a business transaction, I can say with a very high degree of confidence that your wife does not. Remember how at work you paid attention to your company's General Executive Instructions (GEI's) and listened to your immediate supervisors who shared their view of alternatives. You paid attention and worked well with others. You need to do the same thing with your wife. When it comes to your home, your opinion was always welcome, but the choice was your wife's.

Are you are still thinking in your career mode? Do you always think about how much money is involved rather than who, what and where?

A retiree who headed a large medical research organization was complaining that he had volunteered and was very frustrated that the committee talked for three hours on something that should have been reviewed and completed in five minutes. He was in the work mode of getting things done rather than building relationships and contacts with other tribal members. At work, all the connections were given by the organization chart and the objective to make money. **As in the Wizard of Oz, you not in Kansas anymore.**

This change in how you view things is "a paradigm shift." You are not in your big money career world of titles, pay levels and organizational positioning always looking to win, make money and be the hero.

You are home with your wife's tribe and need to think about the first rule in your life from kindergarten. "Work and play well with others." It is not the task; it is the cooperation and team spirit that is important. When you wife asks you to help with the vacuuming it is to include you in her world it is not an organizational positioning move.

Your house is your wife's home where you also live. This is an opportunity to have "a paradigm shift" on how you see your home. It is much more than just a warm place to eat and sleep.

It is the link between you and your wife, nuclear and tribal family and the extended community. It is a place for you to share with others in joint efforts to create a full and purposeful life. In the past you provided money, now it is a place for you to participate and become part of rather than just a user of your wife's space.

Your house and home play a critical part in your retirement. There are several alternatives that you will consider as you move forward:

- Stay in your home
- Change to neighborhood and location that meets your needs
- Start over in isolation or distant community

You can choose a path of isolation and replicate your day-to-day involvement with the home by simulating your work hours. You go to your man cave, garage or workshop and come out for meals. You work by yourself at completing objectives, e.g., painting, sculptures, woodworking, whatever. You go to work and come home for dinner, maintaining the status quo.

You may see the home as a barrier to a happy life, and it is something you need to change out or entirely abandon. Yes, abandon. You may want to sell everything and buy yourself a house in the middle of nowhere. Uproot your wife and separate from your nuclear, tribal family and extended community. You will find a good reason; some common ones are:

- Cheaper to live vs. to stay in the area and locating a lower cost alternative
- People are friendlier whenever you go on vacation, (it is their job.)
- Weather is always better than at home.

- You can get a bigger home for less money (even though you do not use all the space of your current home.)
- Etc.

The effort to move distracts you from the real effort to rebuild your life. Even after you complete the move, you will have to reconstruct your tribal network at your new location, only now you will have lost the possibility of joining your wife's tribe and community.

Your current home might be an anchor rather than a sail powering your second life. Step back and see if any of these are true about your location/home:
- Isolated from neighbors
- Spend all your time in 2 rooms in a 10-room house
- Is your extended family living in another area?
- Where are the grandchildren?
- Are you live-in caretakers?
- The expense of the home is more than you can afford.

If you really cannot afford to live in your home or if your extended family is far away, then a new home selection makes excellent sense.

So, you start looking around at alternatives. You will find, looking at other homes, condos, etc., many reasons why they are not a match for you, such as:
- Too many steps
- Closets not right
- Ceilings too high
- Not close enough for grocery shopping
- …

Then one day, you and your wife are sitting down going over the to-do list, you know all the stuff you do to keep your home in one piece, and you will look at each other and realize that it is time to change, just get rid of all the responsibility of house maintenance. Your home is not just a house. It holds all the stuff of your life. Not just physical stuff, but memories for yourself and everyone in your extended family. Changing it can feel like moving into a hotel room, nice but not a home. Take a moment to experience that how you see your home is changing. The home is the same, your view of it is now different, "a paradigm shift."

On the other hand, your current home is more than you can handle. You still need to move to another house that meets your "today's needs." So, what are these needs, and how do they relate to your retirement?

Location, Location, Location

Here is a short list of issues you might have considered when you purchased your current home:
- Good schools for the children
- Schools within walking distance
- Safe street for kids to play
- Garden area with room for a pool.
- Inside space for kids
- Enough bedrooms - grandparents and children
- Close to shopping - almost daily food runs
- Kitchen big enough for family - room for everyone to sit and socialize
- Washer and dryer in or near the kitchen - do laundry while cooking
- Tub on the first floor - so you can supervise children

bathing
- Closets, closets, closets
- Storage, storage, storage
- Your commute - yes, that is the correct position in this list, at the end

The new list is different. Let's see:

- What to do with all our stuff
- Master Bedroom on the first floor - stairs are of concern, if not now, soon.
- Close to family (children) - in case help is needed
- Close to extended friends and community
- Nearby hospitals
- Active seniors - because there is no one to play with on the block
- Handicapped accessible bathrooms
- Ramps, if needed

Overshadowing your current life are the inevitable effects of aging: loss of physical stability, shaking hands, footstep not stable, loss of hearing, vision changes and overall muscle deterioration. Sounds overwhelming and depressing, that's because it is. Just like retirement, you need to embrace the change. Engage your nuclear and extended tribe and discuss alternatives. Get other's views on other options. You are under duress, scared and, most likely, in deep denial wanting to change nothing. In later chapters, we take you through a fitness program and a change in eating regime, so you can focus on your real needs and wants that you can strive for during your retirement.

Consider this alternative. When your current home becomes a burden, you find a home better suited for your second life. You start sharing the things that will not go with you with other family members and friends so that they can find a new place. You move and begin to network in your new neighborhood and build a new tribe of friends, businesses you shop at, and support groups. Now instead of you being constrained maintaining a home that is not a match for your needs, you can spend that time, money and effort on seeking your pleasures and be involved in a purposeful life.

WIFE - SOULMATE OR STRANGER

"The hardest thing about retirement for a woman is that her husband is also retired."

Through the years you shared common efforts with your wife. These included taking children through their milestones, building a safe, comfortable, pleasant home and establishing financial security. All completed successfully. You are both at a new beginning, and you both have had 40+ years of change, so you are both new people.

Think about it. You are starting a new life, and both you and your wife have been living separate careers that are now gone. You will see how your wife committed all her life forces to your home, children, family and her outside career. Like you, she has given all, and her career is also changing. At this point, the children are out of the house and have established themselves as adults (career, partners, homes, children). She is taking care of the home more as a holder of life's memories, rather than an active growing part of her tribe. Last and most challenging is that her part-time husband is now full time.

Many women have built careers outside of the nuclear and tribal family and do not want to give them up. It is personally rewarding and gives them great pleasure, given their first purpose is well underway, like you, successfully. They have built an extensive network of friends and relationships over these many years, and they are essential.

Your wife has built a life that has time slots for you: Evenings and some weekends. **Ouch!**

Now you are retired and staying home. Just your presence in the home creates an obligation on your wife to interact with you. She has had the house as her space for decades, and now you roll in thinking that you can become one with your wife after 40+ years of being part-time. Your wife has done almost all the heavy lifting of your life's choices. You say, "No I am head of household and made money." Yes, an excellent title like vice president at a bank, but let's see who made the big money choices.

Your wife allowed you to ask her out. I am reasonably sure she even strongly influenced which movies and restaurants you visited while dating. You were learning to pay attention and listen just like in your parental family only now it is your nuclear family, and the chief is guiding you. We like to say that "even if a wife makes a mistake, it is usually in the right direction."

No, you say, you were polite and courteous. It was you making the choices. Ok, let's look at some significant milestones in your life starting with the wedding. Remember how you quietly sat in the back while your wife and your mother-in-law and possibly your mother, were front and center. Every so often you were engaged about bar time or thoughts on the cake. Not your rodeo.

Remember, the furniture selection, again, joint but strongly guided by your wife. You are out making the "big money career"; this is her home turf.

Let's make a short list of choices that are typically driven by your wife. By driven I mean she does the heavy lifting in reviewing alternatives, shortfalls and extended family impacts on each of the choices under consideration. Yes, you are involved, but you are not typically in the lead.[vii]

- What neighborhood your home would be in
- Which house to buy
- Kitchen selection (most expensive room in the house)
- When to start having children
- How many children
- Vacation location
- Religious training
- After school children activities
- Shall we go on?

All these areas that are home-centric, managed by your wife.[viii] This is one of her careers, and now you come waltzing back in, remembering the fantastic first years where you bonded, and the world centered on you, and you want that back. Think again.

Men get the garage, possibly the basement and a room called the "man cave." After retirement even, these spaces are not "safe territory." If you are at home, it creates a demand upon your wife to share, monitor and pay attention. That is what wives do. So just your presence is all it takes. Let me tell you about a couple who packed up and moved to a new state and home and still had to deal with the reality of the home is a wife's domain. Let's see some of the details.

Ron and Donna retired to a gated community led by Ron with the promise of better weather, a community based upon a club membership centered around golf and a newer bigger home. Besides the difficulties of buying and building a home in another state, Ron tried developing a social network like the one he left behind. The gym failed because he was a 60+-year-old trying to work out with 25-year-old gym junkies, he was viewed as a" dirty old man." The club membership was centered around "local groups," and they were strangers who bought into a development from the north. Ron cut back on the gym and found a job as a golf starter at several local courses which got him out of the house three days a week. Even so, he was in his man cave which was located at the farthest point away from the kitchen, over the garage. He said it was a good seven iron shot away. Guess what, his wife complained about the music level coming out of the man cave. It was not the music, it was his presence.

Think of your home as if you were a new employee given a "special job" because you know the owner. Take your time, get to know the other employees and the lay of the land before making yourself at home. Later we have a whole chapter on "Family Reintegration." You get to go through dating all over again, only this time it includes more than just your wife. It is the whole tribe. You are the new kid on the block looking for friends and playmates. This is not your old workplace with workplace rules. This is your home.

So many challenges, nothing like the advertisements. Notice that money is not a vital component of the problem or the solutions. You might say that, if you are forced to continue to work because of financial demands, you avoid the problem entirely. Yes, and that is one of the paths we mentioned. Work until you die, or a medical event takes you out. The other is "If I only had enough money, I could vacation to fill my life and enjoy all the great opportunities I see in the travel videos."

Let's see what that looks like in retirement.

VACATION(S) – A NEW DEFINITION

Overview

Vacations are not what they were when you worked. The vacations were a break from your daily routine and a chance to grab some rest, read a good book, relax and be with your family. Guess what, you are now always relaxing and resting, and you are 24x7 with your family. So why are you taking a vacation?

You still have this list of vacations you always wanted to take, for example, Hawaii, Alaska, and the Mediterranean. Go have fun, make the trips, enjoy. What you will discover is you have been here before. Vacation, again! And these giant ships and resorts built to distract, entertain and allow you to rest and relax are not so packed with stuff to do as they used to be. They have not changed, you have. You do not need a distraction, what you need is involvement.

New Definition of Vacation

You need to look at vacations with a "different set of eyes," e.g., a paradigm shift. You go on holidays to be challenged, feel a sense of accomplishment, meet and interact with people to accomplish worthwhile goals. You go on holiday to get the same feelings of participation and achievement that you got from going to work and your extended community, e.g., tribe. You know the tribes: Boy Scouts, Girl Scouts, and Indian Princess programs with family-centered activities. Oh yeah, that's right, the kids are grown and gone, and now you can't be an old man hanging around young children. Does not fit, does it?

You can, of course, pay for your extended family to go on vacation with you to try and relive the past years, but it does not work that way. You may get together at dinner, but the involvement will not be the same. Yesterday makes excellent memories, but it is gone. You need to move forward. You need to focus on how to see vacations as an opportunity to be involved, challenged, and productive without the downsides of the stresses and strains of the working life.

The successful vacation is within you. It will take some experience, and you will enjoy the journey very much like choosing a job. You need to do the heavy lifting to expand on the milestones and choices you have on which vacations you are considering. The first thing is to stop thinking about money. This journey to help you find the rest of your life, not a break from current experience. It requires participation rather than consumption. You cook the dinner, rather than eat it. You have done this before, during puberty, dating and building your career, all areas where you actively participated and added value. The memory will come back about when you wanted to succeed at something and made an effort to learn and change. You became aware of your surroundings and now wanted to be part of them, be on the team. This was you leaning into new views of the world and changing so you could be part of it, rather than a casual spectator. Step up to the new view and the next twenty will be even better than the first sixty.

Vacations from Full-Time Vacations

So how are these vacations different from full-time vacation? You need to see this not as something your tribe has selected, and you funded, but a fulfillment of a desire in your life. Let's go over some alternatives so you can start to see the paradigm shift.

Short Order Cook in College

During college, you worked as a short-order cook. Money with shared tips was ok, and you enjoyed the restaurant's banter and running the kitchen. You think back to what it was like, and you feel good. So, you try your hand at a few dinners at home, and you realize that you had fun and are interested but not trained. Google "cooking schools" and "cooking schools in Spain" and so many other options. This way you can visit another country, live in the city and enjoy its benefits and learn to be a chef. If it's too expensive, try B&B's, shared vacation rental or furnished apartments. You could even cook your meals in Spain.

You know what happens next, all the reasons why this cannot happen. Stand up and go outside for some fresh air, get a pencil and paper or computer or smartphone and start by getting estimates of costs and availability of training locations, etc. Lean into the process just like you did for your big money career and when building your nuclear tribe. Work the plan, and the method will help you see yourself and find your new purpose. You may find out you want to run a B&B in Spain or be a tour guide or a specialized chef's assistant in a local restaurant back home.

Do you feel the involvement, the energy, the risk? You could repeat this in almost any area you have had pleasure and participation in your life. Baker, writer, teacher, heavy equipment operator are all areas where you can get trained and then find participation in a business or institution in a part-time or assistant role. Remember, in your big money career choice it was more about money and providing for your nuclear family, not your inner happiness or sense of fulfillment. You always had to know how much, and when the job would lead to more money.

Stand in the Face of No

You are afraid of failing. No one likes to hear no, not a match. Remember when you were dating, and you tried to get to first base or any base. I think you ran into a lot of no's and you kept trying. I know biology and passion drove you. Right, you are looking for the purpose in your life. Step back, look at yourself, and give your mind time to reflect on alternatives. Do not consider money, this is about feeling good about what you do or can do.

You want to race cars. High speed drive around a track, not driving fast on a side street. You can go to Disney, and for the price of an admission ticket, you ride as a passenger in a racing vehicle and run the track at 200 miles per hour and go home. An alternative is to find a local speed track and join as part of the pit crew. Pay may be low, but it is the real thing.

Do you see the difference? Can you feel the purpose? Understand the tribal moment of being with the pit crew.

You do not think you could walk up to a driver for fear of

being rejected. You need some practice on hearing no. There is a company http://www.landmarkworldwide.com/ that will help you understand yourself. They have this exercise where you go around to different people and pitch the best idea of your life. In every case, they say "no." No, no, no, no and no again. You then switch to another person and make the pitch, and they say no. Now you want to stay with the success of your career. The trouble is, it is gone. You are back at the beginning, trying to figure out what is your purpose. It is even harder this time because you have no have-to. It is just you and what alternatives you choose that give you pleasure and meaning in your retirement years.

Vacation - a Chance to Play

In retirement, holidays can be a chance to play at doing something that you think can give you purpose. Block out the time, take steps to fulfill a possibility. Do not worry if it fails; you can try another idea. Take a vacation from retirement, who knows when you come home, it may lead to a new way of life.

PURPOSE DEFINED

Overview

A quick review of how you got here. In the beginning, the goal of life was relatively easy. There are significant institutions designed to walk you through the journey, reward you and give you feedback on your success. Wherever you turned, people were there to guide you. If you went off track, they intervened. Now in retirement, **NOTHING!**

Yes, yes, I know, save money and do the bucket list, conspicuous consumption. A spectator sport. Chasing checklists that you need to photograph to remember gets old and boring fast. A real purpose is driven by your soul. For men, it is to provide for the family. For women, it is to see the next generation through their milestones. It is a reason that you might give your life to complete.

Now, with no support, no role models and no tribe, it is a new beginning. The first time you did this you felt you would live forever. This time it is different, it has an end, you die. So, you can wait it out, fill your day with this and that, or go back to work and avoid the opportunity entirely. Many do, with reasonable success. The advice you get is just to sit around and rest. You should focus on your hobbies and, of course, volunteer. Doing nothing sounds hollow, but it is mainly telling you to stay out of the way of people with "real purpose."

If that sounds like a lonely and sad way to end a life, you may want to consider re-examining yourself to see who you are now and if there are things that are part of you that have been pushed aside because you were unsure, or they did not fit into your "purpose in life" as a provider. These things could give you pleasure and satisfaction and a new purpose.

Now you are seeking within to find the areas you passed over or suppressed on the early journey of your life, the one you took to help your family and others. The mission now is not given to you and not supported by everyone around you. And by the way, a few things are a bit different.

Welcome to retirement. It will take some time to start to find and see yourself for your likes, dislikes, tastes, choices of color, etc., rather than what you thought others expected of you. A medical event can make you age overnight. In an instant, the mind and body that carried you this far can disappear. There is an urgency to finding your purpose in this new life. You will lean on your body, mind, and tribe so you can see your way to emotional satisfaction and have pleasure in your second life.

If you choose to live your second life as the first, you acquire stuff, compete to win rewards and honors. This alternative bore you well in your working career, and in support of your family. Many men spend their lives working for their family, and when they reach out to their family when entering retirement, the family has moved on and built their own life, just like you made your career. They appreciate the money and how well you provided for them, but they have their experiences to fulfill. They need their own tribes and relationships to have pleasure and happiness. You have lived separate lives, and they do not have a relationship with you. This is the "Martyr Effect." You have earned all that big money and ask, "why am I isolated from my family?" You are isolated from your family because you left them to enjoy your big money career and all its perks. But when you pass, no one remembers how much money you made. There is a saying, "When your life ends, there is never an armored car in the funeral procession." So, you can continue with the original purpose or take a chance to see if there is another alternative.

What is your new purpose? A purpose, to remind you, is that thing that got you up each day, commute to work and spend all your efforts working with your career tribe to provide for your family.

Starting the Journey to Find Purpose

This new journey is about you seeing yourself in a new light. Not easy. You need to focus on you. You are looking, trying to feel for the activity that can be developed into a purpose.

Just like your career, which took a few tries before you found your success, it's the same here. Except there are a few things that are different.

You Are a New You

We forget that we have changed over the decades. Find a picture of yourself and then take another now in the same pose.

Put them side by side and which one do you recognize? Could it be the younger of the two photos? A little story to show how we do not see ourselves as a new person.

Tim and Sally are married 30+ years. Tim had a successful career as VP in a premier telecommunication company. Tim had already joined some investing and charity organizations. He volunteered to help teenagers once a week. Sally had raised two kids and was very successfully developing her career in learning therapy. So, what could be wrong; plenty of money, both well-educated and had filled their retirement with constructive activities. Oh, the quiet before the storm. Tim wanted to sell the house and move into an isolated community. Sally had built her tribal relationships and purpose where they lived. Tim said Sally, is not the same woman I married, thinking back to those first years of their relationship.

Well, guess what, Tim is not the same man. When they started out in those glorious years, they both wanted a village, tribe, children and everything that goes with it. Now, Tim wants to be a hermit; because the challenges of retirement require social skills and changing how he sees himself and the world around himself, "A paradigm shift." He does not want to or cannot see himself, so he blames his wife for not being the person he married.

After 60+ years you are a new you and the memories of everyone around you are also just that, memories. They have moved on with their lives. Remember how hard it was during puberty to find friends and what activities you could join to have fun? Now you get to do it again, only this time, with no help.

Stranger in a Strange Land
Before retirement, you were so involved with your career. Up

at 5 A.M. coming home around 7:00 P.M. and always thinking about work and very likely doing special projects on weekends. Yes, you and your wife worked together on the home, but it was mostly her describing projects and choosing who was going to do it or write a check.

Now you are back, fourteen hours a day and weekends with all that focus and energy and nothing to do. You and your wife will initially fill the void with home improvements because you both know how to do that, and some overdue vacations. But, it comes down to this, you are both different people and have individual purposes in life. If you are feeling annoyed, frustrated and angry of why things are not working the way you think they should, it is because your mind's view of yourself, how you see yourself, and how the rest of the world sees you are all different. You are a stranger to yourself and those around you. You are visiting, a stranger in a strange land, your home, and extended family. Not as a wage earner, but a retired person. A paradigm shift, you need to see yourself for who and what you are today. You are no longer your career.

What Makes Up Your New Purpose

How do you see yourself? As a contributor as in your past career or you as a member of a group or tribes? Do you see yourself using your career skills or areas of interest to set focus on what to do? Are you checking for opportunities anywhere or in a short commute? Are you striving for financial rewards or satisfaction by doing? The career had you always thinking about your job, the retired you does not have a job. Your new purpose will change just like your career. The trick is to get started and pay attention to yourself. All the looking good, have-to-do's and mandatory accomplishments are gone.

Overcoming the Trilogy Against Change

Guilt

You have had an excellent focus on providing for your family and succeeding in your career. That focus has born you well until now. Now when you think about doing things for yourself, either you cannot focus on any activity, or you feel guilty about spending money and or time on activities centered around yourself rather than others. This is just you, following the guide lines of providing for the needs of others, your family. Allow yourself to pay attention to what you are feeling and focus on things that give you happiness, pleasure and a sense of accomplishment.

To have a paradigm shift, you must think about you. If you concentrate on others and your family members, it is your old purpose. The power of your first career's goal is dominant. Retirement is an opportunity to try new things that give you pleasure and a sense of accomplishment. You have been successful, but that job is now done. Recognize it for what it is and move on.

Traditional Purpose

This is about your choices that must benefit others. You exclude activities that do not qualify as being "ok." Work for a charity serving lunch is ok. Going to a cooking school to fulfill a lifelong dream of being a pastry chef's a waste of time and money. Going back to school to get a degree in archaeology at sixty plus and then joining an archaeological expedition to India to help document a dig? Who would possibly allow you to participate? You will be surprised how many opportunities exist. The trick is not to let your professional training stop you from trying things that benefit you.

Uncertainty of Change

You have all the skills you needed to be successful in your big money career. Even if you have been a supervisor, manager or owner of a company, you are now an individual working with others who are not bound by the rules of employment. Yes, they are free to express emotions, speak independently and look at everyday things from their viewpoint.

It sounds like this does not conform to the organizational environment that you depended upon every day in your previous career. Can be scary and intimidating to someone who has spent the last forty plus years in the institution called work. Let's look at how difficult this can be even to the successful person in the big money career world.

Jake was a superintendent in a suburban middle-class school district. Jake handled all the staff, policy issues and day to day communications of a school district. Once retired, he stayed home and after a year of being alone, finally purchased a dog to go for walks with to improve his fitness and get out of the house. Jake could not bridge to relating to people outside of his career, so he got a dog.

Other examples are Harold, a successful car mechanic who retired, refused to leave his home without his wife Jane, or Peggy the hairdresser who also will not leave her home unless accompanied by her daughters. These very successful people knew a workplace for decades and succeeded. Trouble is once they retired, that went away, and the challenges and fear of failure were so high that staying home and living with a pet was more comfortable than dealing with these changes.

Remember back to puberty and dating. The stress of picking

out what to wear, the embarrassment of starting a conversation and the devastation of rejection. Finding friends and joining a peer group is not so easy is it? But, it is totally healthy and entirely doable.

A Sense of Accomplishment

This is something that makes you feel good. In the fitness chapters that follow, when doing steps, you will feel rewarded when you completed your loops. When you track what you eat, and you see that it is going in the right direction, it is rewarding. You will feel good inside. When you were successful on a project at work, didn't you have the same feeling inside?

Imagine yourself with others, a tribe made up of like-minded people, what makes you feel accomplished?
- Fixing cars
- Clerking in a local store
- Starting a new career as a park ranger
- Tutoring or teaching

What makes you feel good, and you can do it with someone else? You can, of course, choose to be by yourself and possibly collect stuff, stamps, coins, trains, etc. These are things you did to get a break from your career. Do they still give you the same sense of accomplishment, or are you lonely?

Challenging

There is a Twilight Zone episode that opens with a man winning in a gambling casino, having beautiful women respond to his every whim and endless tables of every food imaginable. As time goes by he always wins, and every wish is immediately granted. He starts to feel uncomfortable and asks the concierge if this is heaven, what is it like in hell? The concierge says you are confused; this is hell. It is not the winning, but the challenge that sweetens the game. When thinking about yourself and your new purpose, did you choose those activities that you already mastered or tasks that challenged your abilities?

Let's look at some alternatives that are challenging and not so challenging activities so that you can get a sense of the differences.

In your youth, you dabbled in cartoon characters and sketches. Now you get your pad and pastels and start to recreate the doodles of the past. They are framed and are unique. You spend an early morning or late afternoon creating new works by yourself in the workspace you created out of a corner of the family room or your new conditioned attic or garage. You add a small refrigerator, coffee maker and sink. All the conveniences so you can recreate the drawing of your youth that you left behind to build your career and earn big money. You have rewarded yourself for the decades of work and reliving the creativity that you left behind.

Now let's look at the same activity but seeing it through the eyes of a paradigm shift. You have received excellent comments on your work and are starting to feel direction. Most of your efforts have been self-taught. You realize that pastels just will not let you compete or gain employment, so you sign up for Zbrush Training and travel to Germany for one year to be certified. There you meet up with several organizations looking for people that can work remotely and contribute as part of several commercial projects. You get an opportunity to be a point person to bring ZBrush training to the states, and the team sets you up as a spokesperson and possible instructor once they get started. You work with younger, less experienced artists, and your business experience in the big money career comes in handy when finding all the pieces of getting a stateside business going. Work is not full time, and the pay is minimal, but the tribe is fantastic.

Do you feel the difference? Did you experience the involvement? The participation and comradery of the tribe.

Think about yourself differently, as an artist starting out, or someone wanting to try an art world centered startup business. Do you join or start an art co-op to have a platform for your works presentations? Would you consider going to school to master some new technology that is required in the graphics world of gaming? Might you arrange to sit and do people characters in a local restaurant or coffee shop to practice your trade and get some notoriety?

You say that this is not realistic. Well, the Japanese are working to bring seniors back into the labor force.[ix] They are needed, and they participate in complementary roles at a lower wage. In America, the Amish have a long tradition of staying as a productive member of the community.[x] They view retirement as a change in intensity and expansion of purpose for the younger generation. The Amish tribe uses all resources to be successful. When you live close to Mother Nature, you quickly realize that to survive you must meet the challenges of living. Another view is that to know that you are living, you must be challenged.

Changing Goals

Yes, for a purpose to survive, it must evolve, change, and morph into new and different goals. Ever have a favorite movie that touched your soul? You watched it over and over, and suddenly the magic was gone, and it was just a movie. It is the newness that catches your interest and sparks your involvement. Remember that you have spent the last 40 years with a focus on success being money, title and span of responsibility. You did well, so you are good at it. Now you are retired, and a paradigm shift may help you see your goals not as obligations to be checked off but experiences to be felt, shared and remembered.

Let's look at some real-life journeys.

In college, Jerry worked in a local bakery. He enjoyed the smells, conversations with customers and the physical sense of accomplishment as each of the different pieces of bread and cakes came out of the oven. He was always trying new recipes and techniques to improve quality and production. Jerry finally got his degree and moved on to his big dollar career.

He found memories of the lifestyle and relationships he had working at the bakery. Now retired and 60+, he did not look forward to lifting sacks of flour and getting up 4 am. So, he started by making a few loaves of bread for neighbors and friends and a local coffee shop. The act of baking made him feel good. Jerry expanded his tribe by donating unsold loaves to a local food bank. Once he had built a loyal following, he asked a local bakery if they wanted to work with him and produce and carry his bread recipes. Jerry works with them to evolve and improve his offerings without the heavy lifting. Jerry was able to transition to a purpose and tribe that gave him pleasure.

Your desires and wants from your youth that you passed over while building the big money career still ring in your soul.

Maybe you always wanted to build and fly an airplane. You can work by yourself and spend the time, money and effort to make the plane by yourself or change your goal and join a flying club and be part of a team that creates the aircraft and get a tribe of flyers who share your passion and enthusiasm for flying

You need to meditate on your goals and see them in a new light. Do not set yourself up by just repeating your first life. You are 60+ and have already given at the office. Your goals are not pyramids, they are experiences that you are feeling and remembering with relationships of empathy and caring. Let's take a quick look at the ever-popular bucket lists

Bucket Lists Are Not Goals or Purpose

Bucket lists are marketing ploys to have you spend money. You see them all the time. Must-see vacation spots this year. The must-have sedan. A goal in retirement is a personal experience that is a memory, not a possession. It is something that you want to accomplish inside of yourself, for yourself. Let's look at fishing as an example to feel the difference between a bucket list and a goal.

Is it a life goal to go fishing and catch some fish that you have for dinner or to charter a deep-sea fishing charter and sit in a chair as a passenger to snag a giant sailfish? Think about the process of getting equipment, deciding on where to fish and the frustration and joy of fishing with and without catching a fish. Possibly you did surf fishing off a beach or jetty or went out on a group charter with a bunch of other fishermen. Which best describes an event when you felt strongly about, had memory and shared with others? My guess you will choose the one where you were significantly involved not the one that you were just the passenger.

People and Networking

In your career, the people you were involved with were paid employees under strict guidelines of behavior. They shared a common goal of making money and not breaking the rules. It is doubtful that any one of them would attend your funeral or if you fell in the street, help you beyond calling 911.

People are a vital component of purpose. If you look at your career purpose, it contained service or product for someone else. That's why they gave you money for doing it. Without someone else, you're talking to yourself and living retirement in "solitary confinement with kitchen privileges." The people that will be key to your new tribe are not your nuclear family, they have gone on to create and live their own lives while you were building your career. They will share with you, but only part-time. They have their purpose, just like you had yours.

Your new purpose must be fruitful, and not only has to meet your needs, but also the needs of other tribal members. So, you not only have to see and feel your purpose, but you also must find others who see and feel the same way. In your big money career, this was called "networking" or the layman's version "making friends." You need to try to find an issue, understand it and convince others to participate in working the problem. Let's use some examples; this should be very familiar to you from your first purpose.

You like riding and fixing your bikes. You enjoy riding, in good weather and it helps you stay in shape. Typically, you've reserved this for early morning or weekends. You might even join a senior bike club that goes out on weekend rides in and about your local area. Or, you might have a paradigm shift and treat your interest in bikes as a cornerstone of a new tribal network. Some expansions are:

- Having your friends, neighbors and local group collect old bikes that you and "others" recondition and sell through a thrift shop
- Contact a local bike shop and see if they will support your work and allow you to use their facilities to do the job. I am sure they would like the recognition and community traffic.
- Reach out to local boy/girl scouts and start a bike rodeo contest with proceeds going to an Olympic group of bike riders
- Work with others to create a "Father and Son" or "Grandson or Granddaughter" for 13.6 or 27 mile ride as a family event with awards. Kind of like a marathon with only 4x less effort. Your role is not to win or lead, but to facilitate and participate.

You need to see how your involvement will benefit others. Just like when you were in your big money career, only now it is the tribal networking that is your compensation.

Or, you can pick someone else's purpose and do the things that meet their needs, volunteer work. You show up, do some work to serve lunch, set up chairs or tables, maybe some well-controlled activities where you manage a table or doorway and then leave. This gives you a chance to meet people of common interest, and try alternatives until you find your calling, and this may be a match for you at this time.

Do you see the difference? Can you feel the purpose?

Spend some time thinking about yourself, meditating, to see and feel who you are and what journeys will give you a sense of accomplishment and pleasure. Look at who is with you in whatever activity you imagine, or if you are always alone. The process of finding a purpose is not a silver bullet activity. It is the same as puberty and when you worked at defining yourself. Figuring out how you comb your hair, what colors look good on you and what are your favorite foods, takes time. You made many attempts until you started to see your path. It is the same now in retirement, just keep at it.

It is the same way with your purpose in retirement. Later in the fitness chapters, we describe how you do forty-five minute of steps each day, listen to music and think about you. During this time, you need to expand your thoughts to include people. You need to add details, details, and details. Sense how you feel about them. Remember your career came with a tribe and your wife brought the tribe for the nuclear and extended family. You maybe had some friends from college or neighbors who also had kids. Now you are starting over and need to find the common thread to bring you to a new purpose and tribe.

Think of an activity and the people who you have seen in your last experience with that activity. These are your potential tribe members who you may be sharing your purpose with going forward. When meditating on your alternatives, start with ones you know best and know how things work, like fishing on a party boat, or your daily work out at your local gym. Taking a walk in the park with your wife or neighbor, think about how you relate to these people. Are you close? Do you share other experiences, e.g., going out to dinner or having lunch? You may find you do

71

not have any close contacts because you have been in your career. Start thinking about what challenge will bring you into a tribe of people. Sounds daunting, it is. Remember you must take this time to see who you are now and a chance to see and feel the beginning of your new purpose.

Reaching out to people is like dating when you were a teenager. Pick safe choices like:
- Cup of coffee at Starbucks
- Lunch at pizza joint
- Walk on the local indoor track

You will get the hang of it, and soon you will find the alternatives that work best for you.

Measure Your Success

A little story to help you understand that you need to fully engage in your choices and see who you are and what you are doing.

A wealthy gentleman came to the Royal Society of Science in England and announced he had spent his entire adult life studying nature and carefully recording all his findings in several hundred binders and was offering this tremendous scientific effort to the Royal Society to add to the advancement of science. The society accepted the gift and wrote a sincere letter of thanks and placed the binders in the basement for safe keeping. The moral of this little story is that activity without direction or purpose is just filling the time. It is you talking to yourself.

Seeing Progress in Finding Purpose

"Choose wisely the purpose of your life; you only have one life, do not waste it."

Paying attention and recording your journey are tools to help you think about yourself. What are the activities that give you happiness, pleasure and a sense of fulfillment? These do not have to make money or improve anyone else's life, like your wife, children or extended family. These are things you feel might give you fulfillment. How do you know if you are successfully acting on these ideas? What are the indicators that you are paying attention and are involved?

Talk to Others

How many people have you told about your thoughts? Not your nuclear or tribal family, others who are not obligated to you. You are looking for honest responses so you can see if this is your purpose. If you are having difficulty finding people to share with, here are some ideas:

- **Call a friend or acquaintance.** Yes, just call anyone you know and ask to talk. You will be pleasantly surprised with the willingness of others to communicate. All you must do is ask.
- **Go to a gym.** Look for a gym within 20 minutes of your home and try it on different days and different hours of the day. You find that the population varies considerably. You are looking for other people who can share with you.
- **Join a religious men's club.** You will find many alternatives filled with others on a similar journey. Each person choosing their path.
- **Visit a local coffee shop or Panera's.** Remember the

time of day counts. Get a cup and sit down and strike up a conversation. After one visit you will quickly see and recognize those just filling time. No names or personal details. Ask do you have a minute to talk? I was thinking about "teaching a class on kitchen gardening "and want to talk about it.

Saying your thoughts out loud changes how you hear them, and it is an opportunity for you to listen to yourself.

Take a Physical Step

The purpose in life is like world peace. Kind of hard to get started. All you need to do is anything that moves you toward the thoughts you had when meditating about yourself and possibly abandoned interest. The best action puts you in touch with others having similar interests outside of your home. Have you done any of the following in support of your new directions?

- **Go to a store and purchased stuff.** Yes, a real store, with sales staff and shelves with inventory. Walk around and see all the tools/toys that will help you in this endeavor. Sounds easy, yet many people considering alternatives have not left the comfortable chair by the TV.

- **Take a class or join a local group.** Yes, try any activity that takes you out of the home and in a group of others with similar interests. Could be a college, private training or a meetup where people gather who have a shared passion.[xi]

- **Visit people already doing it.** With any choices you

consider, reach out to others you think are doing the same or similar thing. Find others already doing it and make a field trip. You will be pleasantly surprised how helpful others will be when you ask to visit.

Remember this is like puberty or your journey for your big money career. It takes many attempts before you find your direction. Have you made any concrete steps? Like Nike says, "Just Do It."

Methods of reaching out to avoid

When you pay someone for a service, you need to remember that, like work, these people are being paid to be interested in you. Buying big-ticket items are always useful to simulate relationships. Also, medical professionals can keep you going, but again these people are working and are being paid to be friendly. They are providing a service, not offering a friendship.

You are looking for personal involvement and sharing.

What have you turned down and why?

The saying "You learn more from your failures than your successes" has an absolute truth to it. Have you made a list of involvements that you have passed over? Next to each one, write one or two words detailing why. When people are asked to change, the immediate thoughts are why the change is ill-advised. Does not matter what is changing, all thoughts run to the many reasons that the change should not happen and what will go wrong.

A couple was asked by their daughter if they wanted to switch to a smartphone from their current flip phone. They responded with immediate certainty that:

- The cost was too high
- Intrusion into their privacy
- Who needs those apps, it's just a phone
- Hard to use
- I do not have the time to learn this stuff
- It's a toy for younger people

Get it. The answer was no, no. All very sound and makes clear sense. Then the daughter shared the news she was pregnant, and if they had a smartphone, they could face time with the baby. A paradigm shift. They saw an immediate and overwhelming benefit. It fulfilled their life as parents to be grandparents, purpose.

Remember to take the time and effort to see, feel and examine your thoughts about what gives you happiness, pleasure, and purpose. You may dismiss your next life's mission before making sure that you have seen it from all angles. Re-exam your negative thoughts and ask yourself if they are just instinct or real.

Bridging the Old and New You

Who are you? Are you the career professional, financially secure, a leader in an extended business and family community? You knew what meant success and you received praise, family and tribal support and physical rewards, cars, house, clothing, jewelry, food and on and on. In the beginning, you were young, healthy, well educated. Now you are older, physically challenged and out of school for 40+ years and had left behind the going to work, but you still have that same person inside of you. You may even get an occasional business call on your cell phone.

Here's a simple test to see if you have begun to transition to your new self. When you describe yourself, do you start out with the work you retired from or your current project?

Think about who you are and what gives you pleasure, happiness, and purpose. This time make sure you do not include thinking about the old you, the Big Money Career. It will not be easy, you have trained for decades to think a certain way and now that must be refocused on you, not your career. This meditation begins your journey to your new life. Later we discuss a fitness regime to help in the meditation, stepping forty-five minutes a day, meditating and imagining alternative paths. A change in your eating regime will lower your anxiety levels and improve your strength and memory. This effort will help lead you to recognize several sparks from your concentration on yourself that have real potential for full involvement and a strong sense of purpose. How can you take these feelings and use them to bridge into a purposeful retirement?

Leave the Old Life Behind

Many people choose to leave their old world behind. Impossible you say, guess again, many people's first try is to leave it all behind. Some indicators are:

- Divorce rates after fifty-five are up 110%, driven by women getting rid of husbands. [xii]
- Sell the homestead and move to isolation to commune with nature
- How many people talk about buying a Winnebago and travel the country
- Relocate your home

Recognize that all these merely delay. When done, you are still you, and you may have broken away from the people and community that are part of your new direction.

Procrastination

Remember, denial and procrastination are the most successful ways to deal with life. You go to the gym, shop with your wife, have lunch together several times a week talking about family, financial investing and a couple of weekly vacations. Before you know it, you start to lose your memory. Your hands shake as you age, and you are comfortable watching TV and enjoying your day. It is a choice; we want to make sure you are choosing and not just sitting, waiting for the choice to come to you.

Stay or Return to Work

Go back to work. It worked for forty plus years; it will work for another ten or so until you die. It's ok, a tried and true successful pathway for many generations. It is your flavor, and you are happy. Your family already knows how this works and they have already adjusted. They may, in fact, prefer this alternative. They know how it works.

Rebel, Engage, Step Out, Reach Out

First and foremost, this is *your* journey. Second, your family is on your side. They want you to be happy and succeed. You are the active agent, not your wife, kids or extended family. Sit down and write a little letter or speech that you will give to your family, it may go something like this:

"I have retired and will be trying out new alternatives to feel fulfilled and have a real purpose. New to me, and I am not sure how it all works. I know that I have limited time and there are things in my life that I choose or not choose to complete. I love you all, and this is not going to be easy for me. I think I will be very disappointed in myself if I do not give it a try. Some of the things I have been thinking about, but are not sure of are, build and fly a plane, becoming a physical fitness trainer, work in a bakery, travel to burning man, ..."

Your family needs to have a feeling of your directions. They love you and want to make sure they have not wronged you, or that you will do something that is catastrophically bad. You are also part of their lives that they depend upon. "No man is an island." You have spent forty plus years learning and enhancing your business speak on the job; you are no longer employed. Take your time, share your feelings and thoughts with others. Think of it as networking in search of your new purpose.

FAMILY REINTEGRATION

Overview

Think of this as dating all over again. Only this time the dating pool may be a bit smaller or gone. Yes, your partner, your family who stood by you during your first life's journey have developed their own careers, tribes, and purposes. Yes, this includes your partner, children, and extended family. They all saw your total commitment to career and business to provide for the family but resulted in them becoming peripheral in your life. You may have been home on weekends, but your mind and soul were somewhere else.

Yah, I know someone had to get the money for all the stuff, college, wedding, and business, which do an excellent job of keeping you focused and working. An unintended consequence is that you have excluded the closest members of your tribe. Every relationship takes more than one person, many times several. All sides work, pick up the slack of others, give up deep personal goals and accept challenges that they neither want or need to help their partners. Over time this takes a toll and money does not make it even. The one thing money cannot do is buy time.

Family - Why is this so hard?

So yesterday is gone, and now you must begin the effort to discover and see yourself for who you are. In your big money career, you had help on your journey by knowing what success was; it was earning a living for yourself, family and tribe so they could achieve their milestones. You were successful and dedicated, and your job tribe loved it. Everyone made money, felt accomplished and had lots of new and challenging things to do, including you. Now you are retired. First and almost unbelievable is that nobody out there wants or cares about you. Yes, your value is to bring benefits to others. Now you are sixty plus, physically challenged, emotionally and mentally tired, and possibly challenged because of health issues. Everyone else is younger, faster, smarter and motivated to replace you. If you want to become involved in the working world, it is not likely as a lead or a key player.

The transition is an effort to internalize this journey and start to see yourself and the world around you, not with the eyes of your identity linked to your career, but this person inside you that you must groom, grow to educate and train just like the one you did to earn money. That is the person who needs to reach out and establish new relationships.

So, you thought this was about your wife and family, wrong; it is about you. You can spend 24x7 looking at others and deciding how they can be thinner, more productive, stronger and the list goes on. It is just a diversion from facing the immensely challenging task of seeing yourself for who you are and choosing a path.

Once you begin to see yourself for who you are and not the career personality you were, you need to introduce this person to your family and tribe. Yes, you remember those people who you visited during some evenings and weekends. They are the people that were not part of your working life but made up all your non-work life. Well yes, you are new and so are they. **The dating begins, again.**

Speak and Listen

If you're lucky enough that your wife has hung around, ask her out on a date and talk about yourself, just like you did when you started dating. You need to talk about your inside self, the person you are just starting to get to know. It is ok that you are not sure or have not chosen. You are just beginning, and you have sixty plus years of experience to think about and to remember the moments that touched your soul, and you want to find again. Some things you can say may include:

- I was thinking out loud
- Does this make sense to you?
- I just remembered when

Not like business speak of "Always say it as if it is true, even if you are not sure, so you still make your point." A couple of things, you are not in business, you have retired, and you have no point. You are reaching out, networking to help you hear yourself so when your purpose shows up, you will recognize it. Yes, I said recognize it. You are still paying attention to the old you. Now comes the tough part. You must listen to your wife's response, not with a judgment ear, but hear. This is called "Active Listening."[xiii]

You are going to "active listen" to what she has to say about herself. If you are not sure how to do this, Google it and read a book or take a course, it is how you network when people are not paid to listen to you.

The short course is to listen and concentrate on what your wife is saying. Do not try to figure out how she is wrong or how she might say it differently or why it is not accurate. Just what she is saying. Then say what you heard back to her in a non-judgmental tone, using different words so she can understand that you listened to what she meant to say. Fear not if you misheard her, she will try to explain it again, and you get a second chance. It may take you many tries to hear what your wife has to say. It is not about right and wrong; it is about understanding and seeing yourself and others correctly and not in support of your career. If you have not done "active listening" before or did it a long time ago, you are in for an exciting journey.

Business has yes or no, and right and wrong. Real life does not work in such absolute views. Things can be wrong for you, but entirely right for another. Remember the story of the four wise men and the elephant. It is all about what you can feel and see that determines what you think.

Learning to Communicate is Going Take Time

There is a book "Men are from Mars and Women from Venus."[xiv] It has an excellent discussion on the differences between men and women. There is an example of a husband and wife driving down a restricted road, and as they approach an exit, the wife asks the husband "do you need to go to the bathroom?" He says no and continues to drive. She does this for two more exits and finally says, "get off at this exit I have to go to the bathroom." During active listening, sometimes the right comment is a question. Do you need to go to the bathroom? In business, you are taught to be focused and to the point. Personal relationships are not business.

After leaving the business world, you need guidance on communication, just like you got when you started your career. You are looking for a book title like, "Men from the business world, people from somewhere else." Unfortunately, it does not exist. So, you will have to take this journey without a guide. We recommend you start by listening first to yourself and then all those around you who care about you but were outside your career.

Business people tend to value focused answers rather than process. They look for goals and objectives rather than experiences. Business people not only speak a different language, but they also listen differently. You need to think about what people are saying, not the literal but the inferred, so you can network and build relations. Your nuclear and extended tribes have dealt with you always having your career running through your head, and your family learned to deal with your inattention and absence. Now you are back and need to learn the language and listening protocol to successfully re-integrate with those closest to you.

Active listening to your family will get you started. You need to do the same thing you did all along, only this time you can pay attention and listen. Join a playgroup, be part of a team, reach out and get involved in doing things together. This is a tough change, remember you now have fourteen hours a day of free time and your family all have their "careers" that do not include you. You can become a single contributor and work in the man cave, basement, attic, art studio or whatever space you go to and do stuff by yourself or make an effort to find and join your family's playgroups. Remember you are a team player, a contributor, not a leader. This is their lives, not yours.

Besides shopping, home maintenance, and vacations, what joint activities do you do with your wife? Not your activities, hers. You know things that you do together, and you interact. Playing games like Scrabble, cards or board games. Just like when you started dating and looked for things to do as a group. So, you could interact and get to know each other. True your motivation then was "sex," but now you have just as an important an objective, happiness.

Here are some transition efforts:

- When watching TV, ask your wife how she felt about an action a character has taken. Remember to actively listen.
- Take your wife to buy her earrings, a ring or any jewelry.
- Shop for a new jacket for yourself with your family. Let them pick, you can model.
- Ask friends out to dinner and pick a new restaurant.

Get the drift, you participate but do not lead. These are sharing opportunities where you learn about your family's wants and directions, not yours, theirs. It will take a few tries to build the trust and open communication, just like dating.

What other things do you need to change to begin the reintegration with your family? Simply spend time, pay attention and follow the first rule, "Work and play well with others." A short list of "Do Not's":

- Do not lead
- Do not judge
- Do not have an opinion, keep it to yourself
- Do not have a contrary view

Remember, you were the "big money career" person, and that came with special powers. You are discovering yourself as a new person and your family will be very sensitive to you being your old "head of household self." That was someone they listened to rather than played with. Your family members have their lives that you are trying to join, not change to match your view of the world. Think of these as a new organization structure where you are not the head of the organizational chart.

Remember when you and your wife were learning to live with each other. The changes were daily, if not hourly. Now you both may have new careers, new passions, and purposes. You are both different and are coming together 24x7 again. A chance to live the best moments, not over, but as two new people wanting to share.

Your wife has not been sitting in a corner waiting for you. She has close supportive relationships and knows how to share, and she and her friends support each other. She has a full career, extended tribe and close personal relationships to meet her needs.[xv]

Be patient and pay attention, this is not business speak. You need to learn to complement her tribe, not replace it. Women do things with men, differently than women tribes. Remember the MacGuffin. Pick something you both can enjoy, is with other people and outside of the home. Some suggestions are:

- Line dancing
- Live shows with friends
- Expo/trade shows
- Card games with friends
- Etc.

Kids are grown, the house is finished, and careers are over.

These were the activities that you teamed up on. The challenge is to find new activities you both can enjoy and yet again find happiness, pleasure, and purpose.

Or, you can continue with your lifestyle. There are no wrong answers. These are just choices that you have. The point is you have an opportunity. The effort is in seeing your true self. It may take multiple attempts before you find the things in your life that took a back seat and are now potential things to enjoy. Just like, in the beginning, you have many options, and you also have money, a wife to share the journey and a lifetime of skills so you can be successful and minimize the pain and suffering of youth.

This path is the same for your children, family, and friends. Take the time to see and listen to what their lives are centered around and try to complement and join, not lead or divert.

OUT WITH THE OLD IN WITH THE NEW

Most of retirement is marketing centered around the theme of "Give us your money and then when you retire it will be the best time of your life." You will live to two hundred, play polo and travel the world. No pain, only great pleasures, and wonders. **Retirement, as marketed, is all a big lie.**

In truth, every part of your life that you depended upon to give you satisfaction and a sense of involvement and purpose is torn away. Not only you but also your wife and all the underpinnings of your home, neighborhood and the extended tribe that your wife built over the decades of raising your family. Yes, all suddenly gone.

You have ten to fifteen years left in your second life before aging takes away your physical and mental ability to involve yourself and engage in accomplishing the purposes that give you a sense of pleasure and accomplishment. You can hang on to the old ways, the home, neighborhood, lifestyle, and tribe, or try to see yourself in a new light. Look at the choices you made to be successful in your big money career and see if there are things that can give you pleasure and a sense of accomplishment that you passed over.

Get Started Seeing Yourself

Get started on seeing yourself, set aside the time so you can think about yourself. You need to meditate on you. Think about yourself in your second life. Network with others who are involved in what interests you. Remember, you have money for the rent, food and the time and resources to make things happen. Don't be shy or worried that people will say "no." Think about it, besides spending money; they have already written you off, what else do you have to lose! **"Just do it!"**

Later we will talk about getting in physical condition so you can handle the day to day activities of your new life. You need to have your body and mind working with you. When your energy returns, you can use it to reach out to others to build an expanding tribe. **You take pictures to remember the things you saw; you have memories of the things you lived. Step into your second life.**

Watch Out For the "Oh, No's"

So, you thought the hard part was thinking about your entire life and finding the memories that you can chase for pleasure and purpose. Ha! Wait till you tell your extended tribe that you are heading out to a training school on gambling tables in Las Vegas and your wife has signed up for a semester at a school in Hawaii on certification for massage therapy.

Are you crazy, you will lose all your money! Will she be safe in Hawaii? Is that a scam school and on and on and on. You know you have been successful in your Big Money Career and your wife managed home, and family and everybody lived. They love you, but they have a "self-fulfilling prophecy" that you are retired and need to rest. You are now the child, and they are the parent. They believe they are right, just like you thought you were right when you were raising your children.

Retired people are treated differently. Prove it to yourself with the following experiment. Tell someone that the commute is killing you and you never get home. Watch their face, see how they pay attention. Then tell the next person you are retired, you can almost see their brain shut down in real time.

You and the rest of the world can find many reasons not to do something. It is the instinctive response for self-preservation. Do not argue, just say that is interesting and go ahead and join a forest fighter group or a local EMT unit. You might not jump out of planes into burning forests, but you will be there. They will feel your involvement, and you bring your enthusiasm and skills from your big money career.

If you are worried about failing, don't. Remember back when you started dating and interviewing for jobs. You survived, and now you know both sides, you might find it a great ride and an exciting story to tell the kids.

Imagine someone who retired and thought his productive life was over. He took a chance and took an interview with Apple in their smartwatch health app division because of his background in patient care at the hospital where he worked as a floor supervisor. He loved the Apple watch, and how he could be monitoring his body vitals by just looking at his wrist. He worked on the children's ward and always wanted to make the medical monitoring easier. Apple is looking for knowledgeable part-time testers and quality assurance positions, and he is a perfect match. He is hired to work with a group trying to bring in remote monitoring so that children can stay at home and still receive treatment. He has the medical knowledge and organizational background and he is a trained grandparent and has the patience that makes working with the kids a natural. Who would have thought!

Choice is Yours

Any path you choose for retirement is the right path for you. These last 10 to 15 years are under your control; it is your life. Your nuclear and tribal groups have built their lives and careers doing what they wanted while you did the same with your big money career. They are not sitting and waiting for you. We have briefly gone over five paths, each with the potential to be successful. Now let's look at them in detail.

- Continue to Work
- Make Tasks to Fill the Day
- Grandparent Dom
- Wait
- Paradigm Shift for Purpose in Life

You have ten to twenty years, a nice long time, before the effects of aging start to impact your life. At some point, your body will change and with shaky hands, walking that requires you pay attention, you will need to start paying attention to any irregularity in the sidewalk, so you do not trip and fall. Memory fails, sight changes, and hearing loss increases. A medical event may accelerate these changes. Let's look at the alternative paths you can choose from during your fit retirement years.

Continue to Work

You can continue to work as you have done successfully for the last 40 plus years. You know how, and your nuclear and extended tribe understands, this keeps the status quo. As time goes by, you work from home a little more and take some of those overdue cruises. You get up a little early or stay up a little later and get the work done. Working continues until either aging starts to cut in, making it difficult, if not impossible, to remain. The place you work at is a for-profit concern. Everyone is paid to participate and follow the rules and when you do that they give you money. If you can still perform, then continue as you have in the past.

Make Tasks to Fill the Day

Join a book club, participate in senior hiking groups in the local parks, take more vacations, and work on your hobby in the basement or garage. Visit the gym for two to four hours a day and have lunch out with your wife three times a week. You do some volunteer work and possibly expand your participation with your religious institutions and participate in their senior programs. You live out your remaining time comfortable and possibly taking on additional hobbies and enjoying the home and rewards of your career. You stay busy and can gradually reduce the involvement as either a medical event or physical aging takes more and more of your abilities. As time goes on, you may move into one of your children's homes or senior housing or a "Full Service" community spending your final years with your family.

Wait

Waiting is the loneliest path. You sit at home, possibly you go out for dinner or visit family every so often. You fill the time with TV, coloring books, novels, and computer networking. You have a favorite chair, and when family suggests a change, you have distinct and clear reasons why that is not possible. It is simple, you are comfortable with this lifestyle, and your surroundings, and it is going to stay that way. Any thoughts on change raise your anxiety levels, and you find genuine reasons why things must remain the same. Some of the standard show stoppers used include:

- Too expensive
- I do not have the energy
- I cannot deal with it right now

Your family makes a few attempts but eventually realize that this is your chosen path and they leave you in peace. Finally, you will become physically or medically challenged, and you move in with family, senior housing or a "Full Service" community. Family visits on weekends.

Paradigm Shift

This path is the least certain and requires the most significant change just when you are expecting to enter a time of your life with reduced challenges and expectations of more relaxation and pleasures. You discover that things that helped you forget work do not give you the satisfaction and fulfillment when there is no work. Your nuclear and extended tribe have built their own lives, and in most cases, this does not include you. You feel the loneliness and lack of involvement and purpose, and it is depressing. You try the hobbies and charity work, but the participation leaves you lacking.

In your previous career, you have focused on getting money, gaining control and taking leadership on the job. These are the pleasures you have worked for and received in reward for your efforts. Now, you are retired, unemployed and all your successes are good talking points about your previous life. They have no value to others. Remember when you were choosing your big money career you were looking for what paid the most that you could succeed at. Now you are old, trained at skills that have passed and come to the world with an outdated perspective on how things should run. It is ok; this is what you have been about for forty plus years, ask your nuclear and tribal family, they will tell you if you are lucky enough that they still talk to you.

You need to find out what will give you pleasure and purpose now that your previous career is over. We discussed tools to increase your awareness and focus on just you, yes only you. In the past, you always put yourself last and family first. Now it is the reverse.

The new you must look to see the alternatives and have the strength and focus on making them happen. Just like when you did it last time during puberty and starting your big money career. **The key here is you are no longer looking for power, fame or money. Think about it.**

Find activities that give you the feeling of a personal sense of accomplishment. You are looking for relationships to share the effort, experience, and success. You need to be a part of a community; you need to network. You must find people that you can interact with as a friend and tribal member, not coworker for profit.

So, you not only have to find what gives you pleasure and purpose but also who you do it with and where. You look at yourself and when you see a glimmer of happiness give it a try. Reach out to be trained, join a group doing the same thing, take the time to be with your co-adventurers. Go to lunch, have a beer, work together at your home or theirs. Experience and share without agenda and follow the first rule "Work and play well with others.".

SUCCESSFUL SECOND LIFE CAREERS

If a second life career came up to shake your hand, would you recognize it? You are trained in first life careers so it may not be so easy to see it. Remember, it will be a paradigm shift in how you look at things; they are still the same, you see them differently. Your Big Money Career focused on money, leadership and company profit and successful completion of projects in a timely fashion. So, let's start to raise your sensitivity to know what to look for in this new career.

Team Player

As a team player, your relationship is tribal, not solely for profit. It is the interaction and cooperation that you engage in. This is where you are supportive, and your agenda is to accept others and their ideas, not necessarily convert them to your view of the world.

There was a death in the family, a brother and his wife went to a funeral home to plan for the burial. Things were going along well when the topic of limos came up for the immediate and extended family. The funeral director suggested three. When the brother asked if that was expensive, the director said, on the other hand, two limos would be fine, repeated until down to one. The point is the director took the time and effort to see the expense from the family view, not just his own.

In your next career, you do not play to be a hero but help the team win. It is not what, but who that leads to happiness, pleasure, and purpose.

Make Friends not Acquaintances

A friend is someone who typically shares three things. You have shared a meal in the last month or two. If called for help, they will come and help you and last you trust them in that they speak the truth, they may not agree with your views, but they are truthful. Making a friend can take over 200 hundred hours of contact.[xvi] These are not acquaintances.

An acquaintance is someone you relate to but do not have a relationship with. Some acquaintances you may have had are:
- Gym junkies
- Co-workers
- Neighbors
- Local business providers
- Etc.

Do you feel the difference between a friend and an acquaintance? A friend is someone who after years of absence can walk in or call, and you are at one with that person.

Work with Others

Whatever you choose to try in your second life, do not do it alone. When you worked full time, almost all hobbies were breaks from being with others. In your second life, you are all alone. As was mentioned, a hobby by yourself can be like being in a minimum-security prison with kitchen privileges. You can use a hobby as an area of your skill and interest, but now you need to expand who and where you play. If you find yourself alone, stop and rethink how to be involved with other people who are also interested in your hobby. Here are some examples:

Model Trains

If you want to collect model trains, you need to do it as part of a model train club that has a working train yard where you can participate outside of your home. Google "Model train club." You will find several alternatives.

Collecting toy trucks

Seek a part-time job at a local or chain toy store working part-time to staff the toy truck displays. Work with local Boy Scout troops to buy and sell trucks at a flea market, antique center or second-hand retail where a portion of proceeds goes to a supported charity, e.g., the Boy Scouts.

Sculpture

Work in an outside center and share yourself with another artist(s). A portion of proceeds of items sold then go to a worthy cause of your choice. Network with the artist groups and see if you can join other events.

Gardening

Join a garden club or get together with other organizations for a neighborhood beautification program. Reach out to local business to see if they will fund the materials while you and others supply the labor to create and maintain plant and flower displays. Add a small sign that is visible, asking others to participate. You might even go to a local council meeting and see if support and funding are available by the local administration. If all this networking is not a match, partner with another who enjoys the marketing and interactions.

Political Participation

Look up your local political party and ask to participate. They have all kinds of jobs that will get you out of the house, working with others and many local issues that can supply real purpose to your life. Who knows as you work through the various entry-level positions, you might run for office.

Chess or/and Checkers

Buy chess or checkers set and grab a couple of lawn chairs, and you are in business. In bad weather, go to the local mall and sit in the food area. Put up a small sign "Want to play? You will be pleasantly surprised with other players and the excellent conversation. A pleasant way to pass an afternoon.

Who and How, Not What

Alfred Hitchcock mystery movies opened with you knowing who the bad guy is, why and who is going to expose him. All the action in the movie surrounded an object, a secret, some goal, something being chased. This item which motivates the players is called a MacGuffin.[xvii] The purpose of the movie is to entertain you and leave you with a good memory. Whatever you choose to center your activities around, it is the MacGuffin. The objective for you is the sharing, friendship, and cooperation centered around the MacGuffin. The MacGuffin was chosen because it is understandable, relatable to others and leaves all the participants, including you with a good feeling. You like bikes, how you feel while riding and the fitness it brings you. You join a bike club, so you have someone to ride with, fix bikes with the boy scouts, and run a neighborhood bike safety program in conjunction with the police department. Possibly you arrange for a part-time job at a local bike store supporting bikes for those of all ages who need them.

The bike is the MacGuffin; it could be working on a political campaign, painting, coin collecting, or sky watching, whatever impassions you to share and gives you a sense of accomplishment and purpose. The key is to engage with others in following your pleasures. When you sense a possibility, try it and make sure you include others. It is not only enjoying working with bikes but making and being with friends.

Getting Started - Leader, Follower or Tribal

Your expectation in this second life of your relationship with others is not like your "big money career." In business, titles and organization charts set how we related to one another. This time around, you are looking for a tribal group, not a victory. You try to help the tribe or team succeed. Think of finding an existing effort and joining it, rather than starting one. Getting pleasure and a sense of accomplishment out of your efforts is different than earning a title, getting a raise or having the responsibility for the effort. It is you feeling and experiencing the relationships and making friends that are the big money payoffs.

Here you need to bring to bear your paradigm shift on how you see yourself and the world around you. Do you seek to start or join? Is the goal the accomplishment or the process of doing with others that gives you a sense of accomplishment? Think about yourself and what makes you have the pleasure and a sense of fulfillment and purpose. Seek your happiness and satisfaction to guide you. Be careful not to fall into your old purpose of providing for others and meeting others as a service provider. The goals are making friends, doing things that give you pleasure and a sense of purpose

The bottom line is that you are in the room. Make an effort, be there.

Alternatives

So, you are sitting at home alone watching T.V. and lost for direction. Here is a pick list of "let's give it a try" as some seeds for you to consider thinking about. Things that may give you pleasure, happiness, purpose and create an opportunity for friendship.

The common thread is they require you to be out of your home, work with others to achieve a common goal and build a relationship based on cooperation and friendship. You remember when you were a teenager. Same exact experience, only you are a bit older.

- Sell stuff from around the house in the flea market. Not eBay, you want face to face.
- Collect stuff from neighbors for a local charity
- Tutor at the local school

- Work part-time at a charity thrift shop
- Join an art class and try to sell your art
- Join a political organization
- Find a glass blowing studio and give it a try, then ask for a part-time job.
- Take roller skating lessons and work part-time at the rink
- Become a YMCA trainer - they have courses
- Run a lunch club at a local shop, so people do not eat alone
- Start a dinner club with special pricing at a local restaurant, so people do not eat alone
- Advertise for old bikes, fix and work with local groups to give out. You may get local teens to help.
- Think plant sharing
- Join or start a best front garden in a neighborhood with coordination of town or boy and girl scouts to help older or challenged homeowners.
- Join a flying club and learn to fly.
- ...

No silver bullets, work several at the same time. Let go of the ones that do not catch fire for you. This is all about how you feel, if it gives you pleasure and a sense of purpose. No titles, fancy offices, business dress or income.

Just that you are participating and building new memories and friends.

Retirement: How Not To End Up Tired, Bored and Lonely

FITNESS – EMPOWERMENT

Your new journey will require all your intellect, skill and physical strength to be successful. Remember when you left college and started your career and the nuclear family, you were in the best physical condition of your life. You relied on that fitness to support the immense effort of learning a career and building a nuclear family. Well, once again, you will need your body, only this time it is 60+ years old and different. It has been used for all these years and has stretched, weakened with both use and non-use, and your body's ability to adapt to change is not what it used to be. Remember when you strained a muscle or bruised yourself, and in a day or two, you were back to normal? Well, now that recovery is 4-6 weeks and, in some cases, much, much longer. Ask around about any injury between the knee and your foot, and you will hear three months with therapy to get back to "normal," and that new normal may be entirely different than the normal you had before. When you are older, and you break, many times you do not get back to the way it was. A far cry from going to bed and waking up the next morning ready to go.

You have worked all these years and saved all that money for the golden years, and you are finding out that without your body, the only thing you are going to enjoy is an electric lift chair to help you get up and a walker.

In summary, what you have discovered is that not only is your career gone, but most likely so is your body. The commuting to work every day, office work and time has added pounds and weakened muscles, and you may have hearing loss, and the list goes on. You are facing a new life which will require your body to do new stuff. You have lost your "body" and need to find it again. In some cases, you never had it, and retirement is a chance to pick the body you want and make it appear. We can help you deal with your body if it is not fit enough to carry you through the many years of retirement.

There are two parts to "finding your body," and by that, we mean recovering and maintaining the ability to do what is needed so you can be engaged in your life. In the following two chapters we look at stepping for forty-five minutes a day, combined with using the weight of your body, e.g., arms and legs moving to exercise the major muscle groups, without the risks associated with traditional fitness programs that emphasize muscle stress, weights, and high impact. Later we will show you how to further strengthen your body with an eating regime centered around detoxing your body of excessive carbohydrates and sugars so your body can return to normal hormonal levels.

The result is that you will lose weight, gain muscle and have improved mental clarity without the caloric restriction and physical challenges of traditional exercise programs designed for people ¼ your age.

FITNESS – A METHOD FOR SELF-AWARENESS

Are You Fit?

Let's try a simple self-test so you can have a sense if you are fit enough to retire. Yes, just like you took a physical to qualify for a job, being successfully retired has that same requirement. Not being physically able, means you sit, watch TV and excuse the expression, **"Wait."**

There are four parts to this test. They are all simple daily activities that you do every day. These are not pass-fail. The purpose is to help you see your body and your fitness condition so you can guide your choices going forward. The next two chapters on fitness guide you on this journey of self-awareness and improved fitness.

First, can you get up from a straight-back chair without using your upper body to stand up? Yes, you have spent the last 30 plus years getting into the car, sitting at a desk and pushing a pencil. Now stand up. Not so easy.

Second, try putting your pants on without sitting or leaning against a wall. Huh, a real challenge.

The third test is to walk up a flight of stairs without using the railing. We suggest placing the back of your hand against the rail to steady yourself, so you do not fall down the stairs.

The fourth to sit behind the wheel of your car, raise your left foot and press the emergency brake. Do not use your arms to help boost your leg or hang onto the steering wheel for leverage.

Again, no pass-fail. Just a way to see yourself and the state of your body.

We like to say that we help you find your body. This journey to realize your body includes exercise and a change in eating regime. Not a program that requires endless cardio hours and restricts calories, but one that makes you stronger without breaking your body and that brings into focus the drug addiction that you are facing and must deal with to find your body. Sugars and carbohydrates are like nicotine used by the cigarette industry. This is not free will, it is a chemical addiction that results in you being out of shape, overweight and stressed. Instead of using foods that stimulate your hunger and raise your anxiety, we take you through a program based on science that allows you to enjoy eating and feel at one with your body.

We discuss both eating regime and exercise program that work in combination to strengthen the body, clear the mind and create an opportunity for self-reflection and meditation so you can see the alternative choices that can give you happiness and purpose in your second life.

Exercise Does Not Include

Here, the journey requires another paradigm shift. You need to switch from the "traditional exercise programs" and follow one that is more like Yoga. Instead of running fast, go slowly and change your step pattern. Instead of a period of intense muscle strain followed by lower stress, do not practice any short-term stress workouts at all. Use interval methods and pause so your body can normalize and then continue. Let's be clear on what you need to avoid: the medical challenges and pain and suffering of trying to take a 60+ year body and have it match the training of teenagers.

We recommend using resistance or body weight techniques vs. weight lifting or stress periods. This direction is slower and designed around supporting rather than replacing your life's activities. After about a month, you start to notice that you became more toned, more stabilized when moving and have greater endurance without:[xviii]

- An increase in the risk of an injury
- Risk of aggravating an existing condition
- Stressing your body parts, e.g., blood pressure
- Weights that force your body to rebalance while training and then again when not

Any injury can be months, not days to recover, if at all. This type of training is like medicine, daily small doses.

If you hear any of the following, leave as quickly as possible!

- No pain, no gain

- Use weights
- Faster
- Power through it

Think of your body as a white plastic chair. It is clean, shiny and looks new. The plastic has lost flexibility and strength due to age and exposure to the sun's UV light. If stressed, it fails critically and shatters. You are 60 plus years old, and your tendons, muscles, and bones have given excellent service and have also lost flexibility and strength. If stressed, **they will shatter.**[xix]

Physical fitness in retirement is an activity to help you see yourself and become involved with a support community, tribe, group of people with similar purposes. Remember, all your work acquaintances are gone with your job, and when you look around the neighborhood, you will find that it is child and wife centric. If you are lucky, you may find another retiree to walk a couple of miles a day in the neighborhood or get a cup of coffee. All the support systems, job, tribal community, are back with the producers, which you are not. Think back during and before college, how you made choices of clothing, hairstyles and even how you signed your name. Now you get to do it again, but first, you need to find your body that may be lost, and the tribe to share with, so you know you are not alone. Most importantly, you need to look forward to and enjoy the process of moving. You will see that Mother Nature loves you just to use a muscle and it will take care of the rest. The stress and strain can be left to the teenagers and younger folk who heal quickly and are still chasing stuff. We are older and wiser, so we want pleasure and happiness, not pain and suffering.

Exercise Objective Is Movement, Not Weight Loss

Let's briefly discuss weight loss, so it is off the table as a goal of physical exercise. Physical exercise is not a weight loss objective!

Yes, I said physical activity is not meant to help you lose weight.

Changing your eating regimen will rid you of the drug addition of sugars and carbohydrates, and your excess weight will leave as your eating patterns change. If you do the math on calories burned while exercising vs. calories consumed by eating a snack, you quickly see that it leads to a life of starvation and the forced labor camp of the gym. Mother nature has designed a very adaptive energy-wise body. It is continually adjusting to minimize required calories and building muscles in use while reducing muscles not needed.

Let's look at a simple calculation of calories and exercise. A person who weighs 150 lbs. burns about 100 calories in 30 minutes, when they walk for one mile at a pace of 2 miles per hour. So, if you walk and have a conversation for 1 hour, and then you eat a single slice of multigrain bread with butter, you consume 210 calories. What this means is that most people typically eat more food after exercising which results in weight gain, not weight loss. Exercise is not the principle way to lose weight; it is changing the food that you eat that matters.

Take a moment and look at some video clips of street scenes from the turn of the century. Today, two-thirds of today's population is morbidly obese, why?

When you look back, you do not see treadmills, weight sets, etc., You see animals and people doing normal activities and being in good physical condition. Remember the businesses that manufacture all the equipment are "for profit" organizations. The food industry sells cheap high carbohydrate products that are physically addictive while saying it is a matter of free will and choice and it is entirely ok to sell an addictive product that harms you. They also think it is ok to advertise this to children, to get them hooked at a young age. Eating bad food makes you overweight, and instead of promoting healthy foods, they sell you gym equipment.

Sustainable Physical Fitness – Steps

We are looking at a way to gain sound physical conditioning so that you can choose this next part of your life.

Shoes
The objective is to make fitness part of an enjoyable lifestyle, not a task filled with pain and suffering. Let's look at the steps you take during the day. Just in case you do not remember, this is called walking or moving. The first thing about this moving and "steps" are, guess what, shoes. Yes, shoes. You want to stand on your feet and use them and not be in pain. In all your training for life, preparation for retirement and physical exercise, did they tell you your feet will become soft, mushy, enlarged in all directions and lose tone and padding? Sounds awful and it is. Are you starting to get the drift of a paradigm shift, just looking down at your feet? They were just feet, now they are body parts that need unique clothing and care to be usable.

So, what do we do? Get padded duck shoes. Duck shoes are

broader and longer to handle your larger feet. Yes, after age 40 your feet may require two, yes two sizes larger and do not forget wider. Your ligaments and tendons are lax and have stretched; i.e., bigger and wider feet. If you are carrying extra weight, you will need thicker soles to minimize the impact of walking.[xx] Ouch!

We recommend you look at a brand called Altra. They make sneakers that are zero lift, which means they don't elevate your heel and promote a more natural way of walking. They also come with a big toe box (the place where the toes go). It may take a few tries before you find the right size and brand so you can walk in comfort, and as your feet swell and your steps increase, you still do not have pain.

How Many Steps and How Long

Let's take a few minutes and review walking. Yes, walking, not jogging, not running, not hopping, just plain old walking. Consider this practice for the real work of going through the paradigm shift you will have to complete for a fulfilling retirement. The objective of walking is to use your muscle groups (there are six used in walking), not abuse them. To begin, all we want you to do is get used to walking and get a good pair of shoes and comfortable clothes so that you can walk.

You need to see walking (taking steps) as an enjoyable life experience that you look forward to while you are creating time and an opportunity to see yourself so that you can make choices in your future directions. Think of doing steps as mobile meditation. We want you to look at the step number with a sense of accomplishment, so keep it reasonable. Using your smartphone, load a free application like "Pedometer++," and carry it around with you for a week to see how many steps you take per day. Could be 100, 500 or 1000 per day.[xxi] By the third day, you will be checking and feeling good as the numbers change. Make sure you have comfortable shoes and clothing. Sweatpants, thin cotton socks, and a cotton top would be a good start. Now schedule a time to do the steps every day. Choose morning, afternoon or evening, whatever works best for you. You can change it later, once you start to see this not as exercise but a life experience you look forward to, kind of like going to the bathroom. To help in this, we recommend music. We suggest you listen to a service like Amazon music. They have lots of multi-song albums like

- 50 top running track playlists
- Beautiful - Carole King musical
- Disco Inferno - 30 greatest dance hits
- Old School Disco Classics
- Top 100 Running Hits playlist
- …

Do not even think about the 10,000-step number; there are better things to do with your time. Take short strides and let your arms hang. Concentrate on just lifting your feet and listening to the music and not scraping your shoes. Keep to the daily step count until you start to step to the music. Once you start stepping to the music, it means your muscles are recovering. Remember, go slowly and feel the music.

Most importantly, do not do this for more than 45 minutes to an hour maximum. You will want to do more and more but do not. Limit to one-hour walking and listening to music. Does this start to sound like taking a break, listening to good music and moving your body? Keep it that way, feel that your feet and legs are beginning to be there for you and you are breezing through the walking. That means you can do your steps and when done, go about your life. This effort does not leave you drained, hurting or worrying. Just going for a walk, meditating and stepping to the music. The result is you are enabling yourself by empowering your body to support your new activities.

Meditation While Stepping

Meditation while stepping is the keystone to your success in retirement. Did I say keystone? Yes, Keystone. Thinking about yourself is a critical part of seeing a paradigm shift and the opportunity for a successful set of choices for retirement. If you do not see it, it does not exist. Do we have your attention? Let's begin.

Your primary purpose in life has been to provide for your family by creating and building a career. To be successful at that you had to pay attention, study hard and always keep your focus on the job. Yes, nights, weekends, 24x7. No, you say. You said when you were home with family, it was not the case. You paid attention and had empathy and cooperation with your wife and children. Sadly, in most cases, you were there as a "Dad" making sure they did things the "right way." Love and empathy require real focus and presence in the now. Most likely you were thinking about that project, taking phone calls. **You were meditating about your career.**

Well, now you need to meditate on you. Yes you, not your wife's issues, not your children's career choices, not your money, you and only you. All these other things are someone else's life, not yours. Thinking about issues you may have with your wife is not thinking about *your* life. It is you who is retiring and not your wife. Remember when you were not married, and you made choices for yourself and then shared and negotiated what happened with your significant other? Yes, you get to do that again.   Now, remember you have spent the last 30 plus years thinking about, worrying and doing everything you could do for your purpose of supporting your family.   Before that, your "purpose" was more you-centered. Your body, your clothing, and your moments of pleasure, your haircut, your car, and need I go on? Can you remember?

For you to have a paradigm shift to a purposeful retirement, you must see yourself for who you are and those alternative paths you considered but put aside to meet your purpose of career and family. These were your choices, not bad, just a preference. It will take some time and effort to find the "real you." All the decades and focus on your career, family, and advancement will be foremost in your thoughts. You will want to open your mind to allow your memories so you can see alternatives. Fear not, that is ok, you will snap out with a lap counter click or a change in the music and get another chance to let go of the judging and planning other people's lives and get back to yours. Remember, it is you and only you that is on the retirement journey. It will take time, effort and many, many steps. Remember, **Life is not a straight line.**

How Long Will It Take to Feel Physical Progress?

Let's talk a little about how long this takes. Remember the shoe size changes, well it also includes the rest of your body as well. To set your expectations of timing, let's look how long it takes to completely clear your body of an antibiotic after you stop taking it. What's called the effective half-life can be 50 to 100 days.[xxii] So, we are talking weeks, not hours or days.   It takes about two months for something to become a habit.[xxiii] So do not rush, enjoy the music, and try to make short strides in time to the various songs.

Just like when you started to count steps, in only three days you were looking at the step count and feeling progress, the same with actual walking. The trick is limit, limit, and limit. Limit the time, limit the steps and effort, so you feel comfortable. If you are having a bad day or bad weather, fear not, let it go, tomorrow will come, and you get another opportunity. Whenever we are troubled, unfortunately, we need to find the cause and blame someone or most likely ourselves for the problem. Skip it; it's a waste of emotion, time and effort assigning guilt. Enjoy the steps, music, and meditation, leave the judgment behind.

Counting Laps

When you are doing your steps, you may want to count laps around the track or trips around the block. Another tool to measure and entertain you, a new toy is a lap counter.[xxiv] Why a lap counter? Because as you are stepping around, enjoying the music and meditating on your many life issues including being retired, you will lose track, and the click of the lap counter feels so good, and it brings you back. Surprising as it may seem when you complete the laps and press the button, and the magic number increases, and it very satisfying. Just to remind yourself that boredom is the most significant challenge of any physical fitness program that you will face. You have new sneakers, pedometer, music opportunities of Amazon and a lap counter, and you are just beginning. So many toys and so little time.

Let's take a short break to focus on your paradigm shift. Your shoes now must make you feel good and give you support first, and then look fashionable second. Longer and wider is better vs. narrow and shiny. Walking was to get exercise, now it is to meditate or relax to good music. Walking has not changed, you have changed how you see it (differently). How you look at something affects how you feel about it. Now, let's move on to another enhancement to walking. Can it get any better? Yes.

Stepping with More Muscle Groups

As you start to walk more and when you see the step count it is like winning the lottery, it feels good. Remember to keep it smooth, slow and enjoyable. Do not fall into the marketing trap trying to sell you on faster, more gym equipment and competition with 18-year-olds. Whatever your daily steps are, just by knowing them, they will increase. The trick is to limit the time and impact. You will need the time and energy; the steps are a means to bring you to fitness and start seeing your life and the world with new eyes.

The objective of steps is to use all your muscle groups, not strain them.[xxv] There are two sets of changes that are both entertaining and create an opportunity for improved physical experience. So, we have two enhancements:

- Bend arms at the elbow and position your hands from across the belly to straight out
- Change your step pattern for a portion of each walk cycle
  - High step
  - Raise knee to meet extended hand
  - Walk backward
  - Walk sideways facing left, next loop face right

Bending Arms

Instead of walking with your arms hanging, merely raise them at the elbow. Warning! Warning! Warning! The first time you do this even with your hands across your stomach, it will exhaust you, and you will have to drop your hands. Please lower your hands, ASAP!

Change needs to be done over time (weeks, not days) to give your body time to adjust. The idea is to bend your arms at the elbow and keep your hands across your stomach and return them to hanging as soon as you feel the strain. Repeat once you have the feeling that you can try again. This simple change is pulling in new muscle groups, e.g., your core. The idea is you will be able to use your forearms and hands to keep time to the music. You will also be able to sit and stand with more comfort. Most importantly, you will be on the way to fitness which you can use to empower you to accomplish your new purpose; You know the one you discovered having your paradigm shift during your meditation while walking.

Changing Step Pattern

If you do not recognize it yet, you will see that you fight any change with all your mental and physical power. You say, no I love change. Bring it on. Well, sometimes we do not see ourselves for who we are. Change almost always comes at a very, very high price. You live your life using habit and repetition to minimize your conscious efforts. Imagine if you had to think about everything you did? You would be like a wild animal, fearful of every change, always stressed.

So, while you're walking, you need to engage all the other muscle groups. Let's start with consciously raising your foot with each step. Just a little and only for a short interval say 30 feet or 10 steps and then return to moving with the music. Do that every block or each loop that you count. Sounds easy, but like all change, it is not. You will be stepping along meditating on who you are and trying not to think about your wife's part-time job or how you know what everyone else needs to do to fix their problems, rather than who you are, listening to the music and clicking the lap counter and you will forget to change your step. Just like real life, change gets pushed off by all that other stuff.

Time Under Tension, Resistance or Bodyweight Training

Just for those who like to know how others view this step activity with waving arms and stepping to music let's take a slightly different view, kind of a paradigm shift. Whenever you use a muscle, you put it under "tension." That tension is the same tension that the muscles get when lifting weights, sprinting down the track or doing full body squats, only without the abuse and risk of bodily injury.

When you use muscles, your body generates hormones in the muscle tissue, Human Growth Hormone (HGH), which, when present, repairs and builds muscle.[xxvi] In the next chapter, "Eating Regime" you will learn how what you eat strongly affects every aspect of your body and mind. Fear not, it is not starvation or only nuts and berries lifestyle. It is more of an exposé of how you have become the target of a drug ring. Let's move on.

Lifting your arms and feet uses the weight of your hand, forearm, and leg, e.g., body weight, to increase the "tension" in several muscle groups in your body. When you first lifted your arms, you should have felt the "tension" in your buttocks. You know all the bones and muscle groups are connected. So, using one set brings with it a lot of friends, like stomach, core, back, buttocks, and thighs.

So, you start out seeing steps as an exercise, and the same

activity became entertainment and finally a platform for self-inspection and meditation. That is a paradigm shift.

Fitness - Monitoring Progress

We looked at counting steps as a starting point. Limiting yourself to what you usually step each day and slowly increasing but restricting to forty-five minutes maximum per day. You restrict this because you need all the other hours in the day to implement your new purpose, not just turn into a gym junky.

You count steps, loops, types of stepping and finally body positioning alternatives while doing your steps. You do all this so you do not think of anyone else, only yourself and how you see yourself. You will feel accomplished as you counted. You have pleasure as you expand the steps and body positions for the accomplishment of doing it and thinking in support of your paradigm shift.

The music entertains you, and you take the time and effort to choose that music that moves you and helps you step. Yes, you think of yourself and how it is helping you, not your children, grandchildren, wife, brother, sister just you.

I know the previous big-money career was about them. You have done well, and it is appreciated. Now it is about you and the happiness and pleasure your new choices can bring to you and how they help you expand your tribe to have a successful retirement.

Choosing an Optimal Trainer

Almost all gym trainers get their training from personal improvement and On the Job Training (OJT). That means they most likely have no real understanding of your body and muscle systems. It worked for them so that it will work for you.

Well, guess what, you are 60+, and they are 20, 30, 40 years younger and have no idea what a 60-year-old body can do and what are the limits. Suggest you limit your trainers to those

- Within ten years of your age
- Currently, working with clients in your age range
- Make sure you spend some time watching them work with others to make sure they pay attention to the people they are training to avoid injury.

Here are some symptoms of a wrong trainer:
- Says "no pain no gain."
- Power through it
- Faster
- More exercise means you lose weight.
- Recommends weight training

You need someone who understands your body at 60+ and will not put you in an abusive situation where you may incur an injury. Never sign a long-term contract until you have some experience with the trainer, e.g., a month or so, giving you some time to experience how they work with you. If you start training and you discover any of the above symptoms, just leave and keep looking.

The trainer helps with motivation, technique, and diversity of fitness programs. The real active agent is still you. This book recommends doing the steps; they will help you become fit and help you focus on the choices ahead. It is the combination of using your muscle groups and the detox that give you the mental clarity and energy you will need to go forward in your retirement.

FITNESS - EATING PROGRAM

Summary

Let us remind you of why fitness is key to success in retirement. Remember the marketing hype to convince you to save money and play polo was just that - marketing. In truth, retirement is a very significant change. So, if you resist the change that is part of retirement, all the support groups you have depended upon in the past, tribes, family, and community are very busy living, so you are on your own. Changing what you eat is key to the fitness you will need to make the most of these next years.

We call this an Eating Program and not a diet because you change what you eat. As you bring your body out from the drug effects of your current levels of sugars and carbohydrates, you will move to an eating pattern that is not punitive and never leaves you hungry or without energy. This eating program centers around three areas. First, the evolution to targeting your daily added sugar to 10g/day.[xxvii] Second, target your carbohydrates to 20 to 30% of your calories (25 to 50 grams). Third, 50% percent of your calories should come from good monounsaturated and saturated fats. You will eat unlimited leafy greens, cruciferous vegetables, and animal protein, along with some fruit and fats that provide your body with fuel. Yes, fats, those foods that add flavor and satiate your hunger like butter, sour cream, chicken skin, cream cheese, etc.

This Eating Program is a drug management program as well as establishing good eating habits. Just like cocaine, nicotine, caffeine, and alcohol, you must treat added sugars and carbohydrates as a chemical dependency that grocery stores sell. You need to bring the level that you expose your body to down to the point that it can handle it. Let us look at alcohol as an example. One or two drinks are ok, 3 or more, not so good. Same with caffeine, one or two cups a day great, 5 cups and you get heart palpitations. This eating regime is not new, it has gained a lot of followers in recent years, looked at in many NIH studies, and health professionals are recommending "low carbohydrates and high fat" or "ketosis" like eating programs.

The removal of added sugar eliminates eating anxiety,[xxviii] that feeling that you must get up and eat multiple times. Sugar uses the same hormonal pathways as cocaine, yes cocaine. Coca-Cola initially used cocaine, and when it became illegal, they replaced it with sugar.[xxix]

Look at Appendix A-2 White Paper on Ketosis, that has a series of slides on why refined sugar and excessive carbohydrates are real killers. They make your body old, and challenge your immune system which increases your chances of medical challenges.

We take you on this eating program in phases so you can handle the detoxification your body will have to go through.

- Phase 0 - Get rid of added sugar. It can take 5-12 weeks before you stop feeling the desire to eat sugar, in my case it took 9 months. The challenge is to find foods with minimal added sugar. My sugar addiction was very strong. Eliminating sugar from my morning coffee was the final push.
- Phase 1 - Reduce carbohydrates, to bring weight and blood chemistry to normal levels. If you need carbs, have some, but break it up into smaller servings and have multiple mini meals until you feel comfortable. As you stabilize your insulin levels, it will get easier.
- Phase 2 - Increase food alternatives to stabilize weight and build muscle and core strength
- Phase 3 - Maintenance is just keep eating proper foods.

Warning - Things You Need to Know

This eating program is the direct opposite of the one recommended by the American Medical Association (AMA) and American Diabetes Association (ADA). They recommend high carbs, high unsaturated fats, and low saturated fats. See Appendix B - Background Links for web links supporting a low carb and saturated fat program. In any case, you should check in with your primary physician and have a chemical screen and cholesterol panel so that you can see the improvements in the coming months.

Getting Started - Ground Rules

Before we get into the program, let's review a few simple ground rules which will follow to help guide you in your progress and the successful recovery of your body. Here again, we need to point out that you will be going through a paradigm shift on eating. This shift is just practice for the real challenge of seeing your true self in retirement.

Let's talk about bread. You know that food you use as the wrapper for sandwiches or have with butter in the morning along with coffee, and that makes up most of your lunch as part of a sub. Good healthy stuff, right? Wrong. That good healthy stuff is not what it seems. You know the familiar brands of white bread with all these added vitamins and minerals. White bread had a nutritional value close to zero, that is why they have to fortify it.[xxx] What about all those other bread(s), the ones that are brown and say, "Made with Whole Grains?" Guess what; they are mostly white processed flour, so they are the same as white bread. The people who bring you your processed foods, which include bread, are for-profit organizations. What they have done is replace the regular yeast in nutritional bread made from whole grains with fast-rising yeast that gives you the soft puffy fast-rising loaves of bread made from processed white flour. What you're eating are sugar and carbohydrates. Sounds like a candy bar, because it is. You thought you were eating real, nutritious food, and you weren't, a violation of trust. More about this later.

You know that primary purpose of your life, your career. Well, you once depended upon these drugs to deal with your anxiety and short-term energy needs. Just like smoking, eating sugars and carbohydrates acts as a sedative, (and you get withdrawal symptoms).[xxxi]

This eating program must be simple because you will be doing it the rest of your life. Let's look at the rules.

Rule #1 - When Hungry, Eat.

Diet means weight loss and calorie restriction; this is not a diet, it is an eating program that focuses on eating healthy foods and not eating drugs sold as food. Most likely, your current eating habits come from the drug effect of sugars and carbohydrates, which means this is a drug detox effort and, like any detox effort, you will need to monitor your efforts and progress until you are clean. It will take a little while for you to get the hang of the program. It does not involve you being hungry. Yes, whenever you feel hungry you are to eat lots of good food, only you need to limit your added sugar to 10g per day and keep your daily carbohydrates at 20-30 percent of your calories. So, you can eat all the steak, baby back ribs, roast chicken, chicken wings, pork chops, fish, eggs, broccoli, baby bok choy, and brussel sprouts, with lots of butter and parmesan cheese, as you can eat.

As your body detoxes and the insulin levels stabilize, and your body becomes free of the cocaine-like effects on your mind and anxiety levels, you will start to feel the effects of the hormones your body uses to regulate you're eating, and you eat less to satisfy your hunger.[xxxii]

Think about it. Do you think Mother Nature wants you eating large meals that make you immobile and sleepy? So, you lie down, take a food-induced nap, and get eaten by all the lovely bugs and animals who are hungry? Your body has built-in, specific controls, so you consume limited quantities as needed, and you are conscious and mobile. See Appendix A for eating program details.

Rule #2 - Know What You Are Eating

You know that every food manufacturer is a for-profit organization. That means they make and sell stuff for money.

129

They have found that by adding "sugar" to foods you will eat it faster, more of it, and buy refills more often. Sugar is in 74% of all processed foods.[xxxiii] Think of the food industry as clones of the tobacco industry. They pitched that what you eat is a matter of free will, not a chemical addiction. Coca-Cola says you need to exercise more and still drink Coke. A little story to help you understand the deceit you are facing.

I was in Whole Foods supermarket in the produce department; you know fresh fruits and vegetables. On display was a stack of clear plastic containers with what looked like dried string beans. Reading the label, I saw that the first ingredient was string beans, then oil, and the next was a strange chemical name (dextrin). When I opened the container to enjoy my dried string beans, they tasted like a sugar stick. This product on display in the produce department at Whole Foods contains added sugar in the form of dextrin.

If you think this was an isolated case, guess again. At work, there was a quart jar container that had a label "Salted Peanuts." Enjoying the peanuts lasted a short time. Checking the label for ingredients revealed that the second ingredient before salt was dextrose. Food producers use sugar for its addictive effect and then cover the taste by adding salt.

If you go to Amazon and search on "Sugar Blues" in the book department, you will find many, many, many books on sugar and diet.[xxxiv] Or you can use YouTube and search on "Sugar: The Bitter Truth," and you will find several videos by Dr. Lustig that you will enjoy.[xxxv]

You will find yourself making your own snacks by taking plastic bags and filling them with nuts, pork skins, 90% chocolate, and other safe foods (see rule #3 below). That is because all the fast food and lunch stops sell large volumes of carbohydrates with sugar as cheap food, none of which you should eat because they are drugs and entice you to eat more often and bigger portions. They should be a controlled substance.

Rule #3 - Have Safe Foods

You are dealing with drug addiction. It takes 6 to 12 weeks for your body to detox of any drug. Sugar and carbohydrates are very, very strong. So, when eating anxiety comes, you need safe foods that you can eat in small portions until the anxiety passes. Have as many pieces as you need until the drug attack passes. I filled a 10-ounce bowl more than once with berries or nuts, and have eaten several apples one after the other, in one day. Give your body time to detox. To find safe food, just type in the name of the food into Google, followed by the word carbs and Google will give you portion sizes with nutritional breakdowns. Some of the safe foods that can help are

- Small apples -fixed portion size, high in fiber and sweet
- Prepare one-ounce packages of nuts, almonds, pistachios, macadamia nuts, etc.
- Raw sweet peppers
- Pork skins dipped in salsa or sour cream

Rule #4 – Have Safe Portions

Buy some paper plates and bowls that are smaller and nicely decorated. They should be attractive, and of good quality, so they are easy to use. Add some quality forks, spoons and knives, and now you are set to eat as many small portions without overloading the dishwasher. Smaller the better. After a few months, you may want to invest in some new bowls and plates once you get tired of paper or maybe not.

Rule #5 - Do Not Practice Abstinence

It typically takes eight tries before a person gives up smoking. As with any addiction, you need to lower your exposure to the drug to the point that you are no longer addicted. Sugar and carbohydrates are potent agents. When faced with dessert, take a level teaspoon full. If you need ice cream, buy pre-packaged, individual servings and cut them up into quarters. Take one quarter. Eat it with a "ritual," take the time to enjoy the food away from where you can get more. If you need more, get up and repeat as often as necessary. As you detox, the repeats and how often you need the carbs will go down. Again, this is not a diet; it is an eating program that you will follow to avoid the addition of added sugar and excessive carbohydrates. This gives you the body and energy you will need to empower your new purpose in life.

Day-to-Day How To

How does all this work? The best description is slowly and with some effort because you are changing things you have been doing all your life, just like your expectations of retirement. For you to successfully change, you must know where you are going, see the future. You need to look at food, food suppliers, eating and the social fabric around eating in a new light, a paradigm shift. This seeing of commonplace things and activities in a new light is a tool that needs to be mastered.

Let's us briefly go over the effects of added sugar and carbohydrates as an overview to give you a framework in understanding your efforts and as a basis for you to see food and eating in a different light.

High levels of the consumption of carbohydrates result in a

chemically induced need to eat until bloated and changes your insulin levels so that the standard ways your body communicates, through hormones generation, is suppressed.[xxxvi]

The job of these suppressed hormones is to control your appetite and the portion sizes required to make you feel satiated when eating. They are strong enough that they stop you from over-eating and you can leave food over on the plate, and your portion sizes will change from six baby back ribs to two. You can see why you do not want to suppress these hormones.

You need to treat this as a long run, rather than a sprint. We'll take you through the" detox" with recommended safety foods, ways of handling the milestones you will encounter on your journey to finding your real body.

Issues You Will Face

You will quickly realize that this eating program will result in a significant change in how you see and live your life. Did you ever think that the food you buy and consume and that your nuclear family consumes, that your children eat is laced with drugs to increase consumption and increase sales? The dietary guidelines created and published by the government and supported by leading medical organizations, American Medical Association (AMA) and American Diabetes Association (ADA), are guided not by sound science, but by for-profit groups seeking larger markets.

The objective is to limit the consumption of added sugar and carbohydrates. These are drugs that, when consumed above a safe level, are toxic to your body. They are like alcohol, caffeine, nicotine, etc. We use the phase "carbohydrate toxicity" to convey what is happening.[xxxvii] Once you start to "know what you are eating," you will find 75% of the processed foods have added sugar, and many have very high carbohydrate levels.

Keto Flu

Many people (not everyone!) when starting a low carb diet experience what's called the "**keto flu**" or the "**induction flu**" in the first few days while the body is adapting to burning ketones (fat) instead of glucose. The basic symptoms are headaches. Google lots of websites with a recommendation on how to handle, mainly just eat some carbs in small portions until the symptoms clear.[xxxviii] Keto flu may take several weeks. Do not starve yourself. See Rule #3 above.

Snack Food Everywhere and Nothing to Eat

Let's start small, the area near the cashier at the supermarket or drug store or convenience store, where, almost every product in that area is sugar or bags of carbohydrates seasoned with salt and sugar.

How about lunches? A sub is about 550 calories,[xxxix] 250+ are from bread.[xl] Should I continue with Chinese take-outs like lo-mein or fried rice? How about Italian, spaghetti? A McDonald's' hamburger is 285 calories, 120 from the bun and another 310 from the fries. The total is about 600 calories, 430 from carbs or 72+ percent carbs. **They need to call it a carb sandwich, not a hamburger.**

Very Limited Fast Food

What this translates to is that you have no place to get fast food or even some slow food. You will find that once you detox, you will need far less food at any meal and fewer snacks to maintain your energy levels. There are things you can do differently.

Five Guys hamburger chain offers burgers on lettuce instead of a bun. Choose the salads and fork dip the dressing. Eventually, you will not need the dressing. You will add various vegetables, so salads are flavored. Fried is okay, but not breaded, e.g., chicken wings, love the skin. Salad bars are good places, but you need to be careful to avoid the "bean" salads, which are cheap high carb food. Pizza is okay, just eat the topping and skip the dough. To handle Mexican, pass the taco and beans and order a burrito without the wrap. You still get all the flavor and bypass the carbs.

A Ruben sandwich can be ordered without bread, use mustard instead of Russian dressing and vegetables instead of fries. Great meal, if you pass on the carbs and keep the protein and fats.

Remember, once you've detoxed, your eating will change. Portion sizes will drop, and you will find yourself eating several small meals throughout the day, and just two sit-down meals.

Remember your safety foods. I like to carry a one-ounce package of nuts, macadamias, and pistachios.

Restaurants Can Be a Challenge.

Every restaurant offers a salad, but hot food tends to be a challenge. You usually can have unlimited protein and non-starchy vegetables. Eat any meat or fish and substitute vegetable alternatives for bread or potato. Unfortunately, the vegetables are often overcooked and not properly seasoned. So, you need to work the issue with the staff, they always understand. You will find which local restaurants prepare fresh vegetables in butter and not vegetable oil and eating out tends to be more enjoyable once you locate a restaurant that will cook vegetables in a way that they are not overcooked. You will be pleasantly surprised how cooperative they can be.

If you are going to have a starch, baked or French-fried potato or sweet potato, have them put it on a separate plate and cut it up in quarters and take only one quarter at a time. Denial is not the objective, limited quantities are. Enjoy, just don't eat the whole thing. Once detox is over, it becomes much easier to enjoy meat and vegetables and small portions of carbohydrates.

Dessert

Yes, either at home or eating out you want a sweet dessert. I do, too. Use your teaspoon and help yourself to one level teaspoon of one or as many desserts as you need. You will need less and less as the eating anxiety associated with overdosing on added sugar wanes.

Even better, select fresh blueberries, blackberries and/or raspberries, and have them put several tablespoons of sour cream or plain yogurt as a topping. Sugar is an active drug so it will take time to break the habit.

Let me tell you a story about Linda. She had an autoimmune disease, psoriasis, which commonly results in dry, raised, red skin lesions (plaques) covered with silvery scales. Linda had a 30% coverage over her body, significant coverage. There is a strong association with added sugar in the diet and outbreaks of psoriasis. Strong motivation not to eat sugar. The bottom line is that Linda had ice cream every night because she "needed it." Do you feel the addiction?

Fatty Cuts of Meat Hard to Find

Now you can eat fatty meats, so you will enjoy a pork chop or pastrami sandwich with fat on the meat so when cooked you get the full flavor, and it satisfies your hunger. The problem will be that supermarkets and butchers have lean pork chops with no fat. You will have to hunt down the less expensive cuts of meat like pork rib end chops or shoulder that are marbled with fat, and when you taste the difference, you will understand why Mother Nature wants you to eat that way, so your body has a good energy source.[xli]

Boring

You start eating baby back ribs (without the sweet sauce), chicken wings, steak, lamb chops with non-starchy vegetables covered in butter. You may add garlic and grated parmesan cheese to kick up the veggies. You expand on the meat dishes with mayonnaise, and other non-sugar-based dry rubs and sauces. In any case, as time goes on, even this eating becomes **BORING.**

You need to become "champion of your food." Just to bring you back, you need to know what you want, how you want to feel when you eat. Drug addicts go back to being drug users.[xlii] I remind you that added sugar is using the same biological mechanism as cocaine, and detox is a long-term effort.[xliii] You have used food to meet the demands of your purpose, your career. Now you need to start "seeing" food to find and live your new life. Eating this way is not to lose weight, it is to clear your body of drug addiction so that you can live your life.

You need to find your purpose and avoiding the tell-tale symptoms of a relapse.[xliv] Notice the first item under emotion is isolation; you need a tribe. Do you see a paradigm shift? It is who you eat with and where that determines if you are fulfilling your new purpose.

The following is a punch list of symptoms that are indicators that you are relapsing. Replace the word "drug" with "sugar" or food with carbs.   If you find yourself thinking or saying some of the following:

- Eating a dessert is ok. It helps me relax
- I do not feel a meal is complete without something sweet
- Just a little cheat
- Just one drink for the road

The drug addictive properties are you talking to you. Sugar is a drug with additive powers and not just a matter of choice and free will. You are in the ring with an 800-pound gorilla who is funded and supported by the trillion-dollar food industry. The following bullet list is to help drug addicts become aware they are possibly relapsing. It is broken up into emotional, mental and physical lists:

Emotional
- Isolating oneself
- Not going to treatment or meetings
- Going to meetings but not sharing
- Bottling up emotions
- Poor eating and sleeping habits
- Not taking care of self mentally or physically
- Denial
- Relaxing of self-imposed rules

Mental
- Drug cravings
- Thinking about people and places associated with past drug use
- Romanticizing past drug use

- Minimizing consequences
- Bargaining with self
- Lying to others
- Thinking about how to control drug use next time
- Planning a relapse or looking for opportunities

Physical
- Using drugs "just once."
- Returning to uncontrolled use

Does this sound like you when looking at dessert alternatives? You need to feel and see yourself so that you can choose the path going forward. The excessive sugar and carbs are drugs used to keep your consumption of product up and to hide low-quality product. If you have these thoughts, it is a warning you are returning to a drug-induced state. Pay attention, choose a path.

Tools to Help You Know Who You Are and What Makes You

In the step exercise program, we mentioned counting laps and seeing the numbers change as a reward unto itself. **If you can see it, you can feel it, and it is part of your life.**

These tools/toys give visibility and focus to your eating program. It makes things more interesting, and the information provides re-enforcement, especially if you are doing this program alone. Tracking your progress helps you to stay on program and avoid eating the wrong foods due to not paying attention. Remember the food industry actively fights truth in labeling, e.g., added sugar as a separate item in food content. They are in it for profit, not your well-being. You need to pay attention.

These tools/toys are almost a must to be successful. Remember you have been living a purposeful life providing for your family and growing your career. In many cases, your body took second place, and it developed a direction on its own, very similar to your wife. During your youthful years, you courted your body and worked to make it shiny and attractive, e.g., puberty. You get to do this again, only now it is so you can have the resources to achieve your new purpose. This time many support people and groups are missing. Now, you do not have all those hormones, family tribe members, institutions and tribal leaders to guide you.

Let's look at the first tool that supports you knowing what you eat.

MyFitnessPal

An app for your smartphone that allows you to enter what you eat and display the number of calories, carbohydrates, fat and protein in one of several different displays. The app gives you an easy and quick way to measure the percent carbohydrates or grams of carbs to make sure you are staying within the selected limits. The product website has extensive descriptions, and the free version is very comprehensive.[xlv] Let's talk about its use in your journey to find your new purpose.

Your need for energy and good general fitness is a critical component for you to be able to do the mental and physical work like what you went through during puberty and in building your career. So, what is happening by limiting carbohydrates and added sugar?

In brief, your insulin levels stabilize, and your body switches over to using fats and proteins to fuel your cell energy requirements. Also, Human Growth Hormone (HGH) levels increase, and two known appetite control hormones start to control and participate in your food consumption.[xlvi] It can take place six to twelve weeks as your body detoxes.

The HGH will result in increased muscle growth. As you use your muscles, and they go under tension, this hormone grows the muscle. The appetite hormones will result in significant reduction of the quantity of food required to give you a satiated feeling and stop you from overeating.[xlvii]

Given that the food industry has chosen to create 60+% of processed products with added sugars and carbohydrates, knowing what you are eating seems to be a reasonable effort that results in significant benefits.[xlviii]

The benefits of the app can address the boredom, clerical effort and complexity of manually tracking food consumption. The app makes monitoring food eaten almost a game that has many options for sharing, customization, and personalization that makes its use ever involving and almost entertainment, e.g., eye candy.

An additional benefit of MyFitnessPal is that it inter-works with several other apps that you can use. One we recommend is "Connect" which uses the Garmin Vivo Active 3 Smartwatch.

Garmin Vivo Active 3 Smart Watch with Connect

In the spirit of seeing who you are, you can expand your awareness of self in support of finding your new purpose by knowing more about your physical person. A smartwatch, such as the Garmin Vivo Active 3, has many of the features you need to get to know yourself. Many YouTube videos and websites cover both the intro and detail of this fantastic tool/toy. Here is a short list of things you get to know about yourself, just by wearing the watch:

- Number of steps even when you do not have your phone with you
- Number of stairs up and down
- Hours slept, both deep and shallow, along with a full history
- Heart rate. An easy way to know your heart rate. Very handy when doing interval training, e.g., how long an interval is required to bring your heart rate down.
- A quantitative measure of stress level
- A V02 measure of fitness (requires a short walk)

To avoid the killer of any fitness program, boredom, you need to be aware, so you can make it part of your life. The watch brings all these sparkly measurements that you can track, compare with others and remind yourself of the significant progress you are making in finding yourself. Another nice feature is that it inter-works with MyFitnessPal, so all your exercise is included when calculating your calorie requirements and usage. The objective is not to limit calories; your body will do that for you. It is for you to know how much and what you are eating. **Knowledge is power.**

Weight Watchers Scale and Weight Watchers App

As you detox and you're eating habits start to change, you can measure your key metrics on the state of your body with a single activity, stepping on the scale. You get the following tracked for you:

- Weight
- BMI

- Muscle
- Bone
- Water
- Fat

The Weight Watchers scale does this by passing a mild current (you do not feel it) through your feet and using a magic algorithm to give you these metrics. The app has these lovely graphs to show you trends on how you are doing. Yes, yes there are better, more accurate tools to get these measurements, but it is the trend we are looking for to entertain you and keep you involved with your body and life.

Detox - Eating Regime Monitoring Progress

Again, the eating regime brings focus to you. Limiting sugar and carbohydrates is a drug detox effort, yes drug detox. This effort is to raise your awareness of your choices and how they impact how often and how much of these drugs you are consuming. MyFitnessPal, a smartphone application makes recording fast, entertaining and straightforward. As you progress, you can easily see if you need more carbs, protein or fats to meet your percentages. As with any drug addiction, it typically takes multiple tries; smokers try to quit at least eight times before being successful, as part of the self-awareness. This eating regime is not one of abstinence. Use safe foods and record them. Take small portions and come back if you need another. Keep track of all eating. The recording will help you be aware of yourself and give you a better view of who you are.

You may see in your new eating regime a purpose of your retirement. How you feel about it, how you view your ups and downs of mastering clean eating habits and using the moment to guide you to build a network of people that can benefit from your experience and feelings. Having to provide foods and prepare them not to feed an addiction, but the choice of how things taste and how they make you feel may lead you to be part of a kitchen or a restaurant specializing in healthy menus.

By weighing yourself with the Weight Watchers scale, you will see the weight changes. Inspect your body and notice your muscles will start to grow once your insulin levels have stabilized, your body will produce the HGH needed for muscle growth. Might this lead to coaching a team that was part of your childhood that you left behind for your big money career? Or might it open a new area of personal physical fitness that you always wanted to do, but did not have the time or focus on starting or completing? Now you could become a certified trainer and work at a gym specializing in fitness for seniors. Your expanded tribe could be other trainers, etc. all giving value to the senior community. Measuring your food, weight, and fitness brings focus and opportunity to think if this is a purpose that touches your soul.

BRINGING IT ALL TOGETHER

This book started with the recognition of the marketing lie that all you need to do to have a successful retirement is invest your savings.   It turns out that money is only one part of the challenge of a successful retirement.

We saw how the support you expected, the same you experienced on your journey to your Big Money Career, disappeared once you retired. The tribe you depended upon from work were acquaintances rather than friends, and once you no longer worked together, they became strangers. Your nuclear family members have built their own lives while you were at work, and when you try to come back home, you are a stranger and need to rebuild your relationships with those who you just spent your life's purpose supporting.

You might get 12 to 24 months of fixing up the house, going on the missed vacations and adjusting to not going to work. Then the lack of purpose leaves you bored, alone and physically exhausted.

We journeyed through each of the major parts of your life, home, spouse, vacations, and purpose to see the impact of retirement. We looked at the different paths that you may choose and worked through the alternative path of "a paradigm shift" as a way of seeing yourself and the world around you through different eyes. The goal is to see and experience pleasure, happiness, and purpose in retirement. This shift requires meditation so you can see yourself living the possible opportunities you passed over during your Big Money Career. Recognize that the successful rules of your working life need to change for retirement.

We covered examples that showed the key is not what you do, as in your career, but you need to be with friends, outside of your house and as a supportive team member working together in support of a MacGuffin, that thing that gives you pleasure and happiness to work on.

We then covered two areas that are critical in experiencing your second life, retirement: (1) fitness so you can have the wherewithal to do things, and (2) an eating regime so your body can detox from the food-based drugs you used to empower your career. This eating regime supports your body in building muscle, removes the anxiety and stress induced by sugar and carbohydrates, and enables you to use food as the fuel to give you energy, rather than as a mechanism to induce you to eat and buy more products. At the same time, make your fitness program an opportunity to meditate and see yourself not as a provider, but as a person seeking pleasure, happiness, and purpose in the things you do for yourself. Yes, meditate on yourself, not anyone else.

Any of the alternative paths you choose for your retirement are valid. The purpose of this book is to raise your awareness of the alternatives so you can make a conscious choice on how you want to spend your second life.

How do you begin this journey of success? We recommend you start by evaluating your fitness and embrace a good eating regime, so you can have the energy and strength to live your second life.

The challenge for you is to become an empowered person, a person who actively listens, getting to know your family who has also changed over these last 40+ years. Learn to value the experience, memories, and friendships rather than money and goals. **This is your life, you have worked hard, enjoy it.**

Retirement: How Not To End Up Tired, Bored and Lonely

148

APPENDICES

APPENDIX A-1 EATING PROGRAM SAMPLE MENU

There are many services available that detail low carb, high-fat eating regimes or "ketosis" programs. If you Google "Low carb high-fat diet" you will see many alternatives. We recommend you use MyFitnessPal to monitor your eating program and help you guide your selections as you get a feel for what you are eating, vs. what you think you are eating. Following is a sample menu of meal options on a typical day to give you an idea of the types of foods that you can eat.

Your body, as it detoxes from the carbohydrates and anxiety of added sugars, you will reduce the amount you eat[xlix]

Google Search Keywords

Low carbs and high fat or "Ketosis" eating regimes have many, many advocates. It goes contrary to the current AMA and ADA recommendations so that you can imagine the number of non-supportive listings. Here are some keywords to help you in your searches.

- NIH - National Institute of Health added to any other words will bring up actual research

- Carbohydrate toxicity -
- Ketosis -
- Added Sugar

Sample Menu

Typical Eating Day - 4 to 6 mini meals Heavy on butter and mayo

1. Breakfast - sometimes eaten as two meals 5-6 AM and then another at 9 or 10 AM
   a. 1-2 cups coffee with half and half with ½ avocado
   b. Fried egg in butter with greens and two pieces of bacon
   c. Two tablespoons of whole Greek yogurt with cooked 2-3 figs or 3-4 cooked prunes
2. Lunch
   a. Bowl of salad with 2-3 chicken wings with mayonnaise
   b. Frozen vegetable pack with lightly salted butter, parmesan cheese
   c. 1-3 ribs no sauce
   d. Chicken wings with mayonnaise
   e. Five Guys hamburger wrapped in lettuce
3. Diner
   a. Fish, ribs, liver, dark meat chicken
   b. Pork chops – Rib end cut
   c. Frozen vegetables pack with real butter
   d. ½ small sweet potato.
4. Snacks
   a. Water 8 -12 cups per day
   b. 12 oz cup of chicken or beef bone broth
   c. Small raw sweet peppers
   d. Carrot and piece of cheese

e. 12-ounce bowl pork rinds

f. 12-ounce bowl cut watermelon

g. ½ cup frozen raspberries, blackberries or blueberries with two tablespoons of sour cream

h. Late night snack to help sleep ¼ Klondike bar (as needed)

i. Square of dark chocolate 70 to 90% chocolate

j. ½ avocado snack

APPENDIX A-2 KETOSIS WHITE PAPER
P.J. Smith presentation to Mensa meeting 2018

The Science for the Low-Carb Diet

THE SCIENCE FOR THE LOW-CARB DIET

How carbohydrates destroy our health,
and how we can get it back.

The human body is amazingly adaptable when it comes to food. As omnivores, we can eat almost anything and survive. But surviving does not always mean thriving.

What we eat matters. Our bodies are complex biochemical systems that work hard to maintain a perfect environment for our cells and organs to function. But when we feed them things that throw that homeostasis out of balance, we suffer the consequences.

How Sick Are We?

150m
Diabetes or
Pre-Diabetes

175m
Overweight or
Obese

92m
Cardiovascular
Disease

86m
High Blood
Pressure

44m
Osteoporosis or
Low Bone Mass

Statistics from: https://www.cdc.gov/diabetes/pdfs/data/statistics/national-diabetes-statistics-report.pdf,https://www.iofbonehealth.org/facts-statistics, https://www.cdc.gov/nchs/fastats/obesity-overweight.htm, https://healthmetrics.heart.org/wp-content/uploads/2017/06/Heart-Disease-and-Stroke-Statistics-2017-ucm_491265.pdf

A 2017 CDC report revealed that at least 150 million people have diabetes or pre-diabetes.

175 million adults are overweight or obese. 92 million adults are living with some form of cardiovascular disease. 86 million have high blood pressure. 25 percent have the non-alcoholic fatty liver disease.

44 million have osteoporosis or low bone mass.

What do all these diseases have in common? They are known as "lifestyle diseases" or more classically, "the diseases of civilization." They have been around since the invention of agriculture. But they are not inevitable.

Note: Slide Statistics from: https://www.cdc.gov/diabetes/pdfs/data/statistics/national-diabetes-statistics-report.pdf,https://www.iofbonehealth.org/facts-statistics, https://www.cdc.gov/nchs/fastats/obesity-overweight.htm, https://healthmetrics.heart.org/wp-content/uploads/2017/06/Heart-Disease-and-Stroke-Statistics-2017-ucm_491265.pdf

Hunters vs Farmers

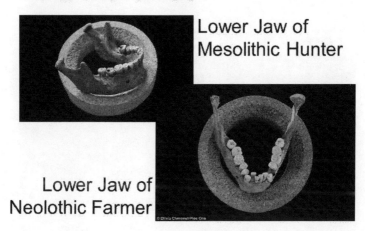

Lower Jaw of
Mesolithic Hunter

Lower Jaw of
Neolothic Farmer

When we look at the heath of hunter-gatherer communities such as Australian Aborigines and North American Inuit, we find these diseases almost absent. No diabetes, no obesity or heart disease.

When we look at the archeological record, we see a sharp divide between the hunter/gatherer communities and the agricultural civilizations that follow, with a dramatic decline in health. Hunter-gatherers had better bones, had no signs of iron-deficiency anemia, no signs of infection, few (if any) dental cavities, fewer signs of arthritis and were in general larger and more robust than their agriculture-following contemporaries.

In the book Pandora's Seed: The Unforeseen Cost of Civilization, genetic anthropologist Spencer Wells writes of the change to agriculture: "Strikingly, the measures of health decrease dramatically. Male height drops from nearly five foot ten in the Paleolithic to approximately five-three in the Late Neolithic. People were not only dying younger; they were dying sicker. Overall, the data show that the transition to an agricultural lifestyle made people less healthy."

How Did We Get Here?

- 1963: Diet-Heart Hypothesis
- 1960s: "The sugar industry paid scientists to play down the link between sugar and heart disease and promote saturated fat as the culprit." (NY Times)
- 1977: USDA: Low-fat, high-carb diet

https://www.nytimes.com/2016/09/13/well/eat/how-the-sugar-industry-shifted-blame-to-fat.html

So these diseases have been with us since the invention of agriculture. But the overwhelming prevalence that we are experiencing now is something relatively new. It is caused primarily by the standard American diet: a diet toxically high in carbohydrates and polyunsaturated fats. How did we get here? In the first half of the 20th century, there was much debate over the causes of heart disease. Some thought it was caused by fat and cholesterol, while others blamed carbohydrates and triglycerides.

One scientist, Ancel Keys, proposed the Diet-Heart Hypothesis in 1963. It predicted that replacing saturated fat with vegetable oil rich in linoleic acid would reduce coronary heart disease events and deaths by lowering serum cholesterol. Keys produced a longitudinal epidemiological study called the Seven Countries Study to back this up, but later analysis revealed that he had cherry-picked and falsified his data to fit his hypothesis.

Keys lied, and more importantly, he lied to the right people at the right time to impose his beliefs on the American people and the world. A recent New York Times report revealed that during the 1960s, the sugar industry was busy paying scientists to play down the link between sugar and heart disease and promote saturated fat as the culprit instead.
Note: Slide Reference: https://www.nytimes.com/2016/09/13/well/eat/how-the-sugar-industry-shifted-blame-to-fat.html

The Low-Fat Food Pyramid

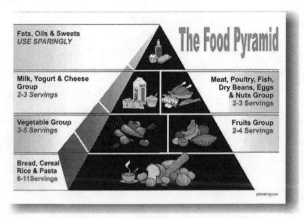

One of those scientists was D. Mark Hegsted, who went on to become the head of nutrition at the United States Department of Agriculture, wherein 1977 he helped draft the forerunner to the federal government's dietary guidelines. Another was Dr. Fredrick J. Stare, the chairman of Harvard's nutrition department.

With the backing of government organizations, the low-fat, high-carbohydrate diet became gospel, despite the fact that science never supported it.

High Sugar Intake

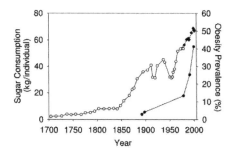

Source: Johnson RJ, et al. Potential role of sugar (fructose) in the epidemic of hypertension, obesity and the metabolic syndrome, diabetes, kidney disease, and cardiovascular disease. The American Journal of Clinical Nutrition, 2007.

The sugar industry took full advantage of this, and as fat was removed from foods, sugar was added. We now are consuming vast amounts of sugar, higher than any point in history.

Note: Slide Source: Am J Clin Nutr. 2007 Oct;86(4):899-906. **Potential role of sugar** (fructose) in the epidemic of hypertension, obesity and the ... **Johnson** RJ(1), Segal MS, Sautin Y, Nakagawa T, Feig DI, Kang DH, Gersch MS, Benner S, Sánchez-Lozada LG.

400+ Extra Calories Per Day

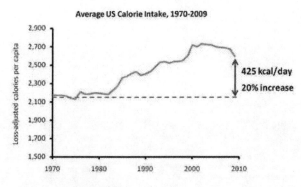

Source: Dr. Stephan Guyenet. The American Diet, 2012.

That sugar makes us hungrier. We are eating not only more sugar but more calories overall.

Note: Slide source: EDxHarvardLaw - Stephan **Guyenet** - The **American Diet**. TEDx Talks 2012

Low-Fat Made Us Fat

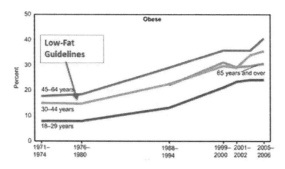

Source: National Center for Health Statistics (US). Health, United States, 2008. With Special Feature on the Health of Young Adults. Hyattsville (MD): National Center for Health Statistics (US); 2009 Mar. Chartbook.

In consequence, we now have a population in a health crisis.

So what is the science behind these health issues, and what can we do to stop or even reverse them? For decades, health officials have said the same thing: a low-fat diet and exercise. Cut back on portion sizes. Use your willpower. On the surface, sensible ideas. But study after study has shown that they don't work.

Because this isn't about willpower. It's about insulin.

Note: Slide Source: National Center for Health Statistics (NCHS)Health, United States, 2008 With Special Feature on the Health of Young Adults. National Center for Health Statistics (US) . Hyattsville (MD): National Center for Health Statistics (US); 2009 Mar. Chartbook

The Power of Insulin

> **All carbohydrates, including whole grains, become sugar**

> **Insulin lowers blood sugar**

> **Every high-carb meal is a crisis**

Insulin is a powerful hormone. One of its main roles is to regulate our blood sugar. If our bodies couldn't make insulin -- a condition is known as type 1 diabetes -- what would happen when we ate a typical American meal, loaded with carbohydrates? Our blood sugar would skyrocket. High blood sugar is toxic to the body. It damages our heart, nerves, and kidneys. It causes problems in our bones, joints, and skin. Our teeth and gums become infected, our eyes cloud with cataracts, and poor circulation can lead to amputations. Without insulin to stop it, sugar will rot us from the inside.

But insulin protects us. Every time we eat, as our blood sugar increases so does our insulin. Within an hour of eating, it can remove all the extra glucose from our bloodstream and store it safely away in our muscles, liver, and fat tissue. Blood sugar levels drop back to their homeostatic level: crisis averted. But most people eat at least three meals a day, plus one or more snacks. And in the typical American diet, every one of those meals and snacks is primarily carbohydrates. Worse, they are refined carbohydrates: flour, sugar, corn syrup, fruit juice, potatoes. These cause blood sugar to spike even higher.

The High-Carbohydrate Cycle

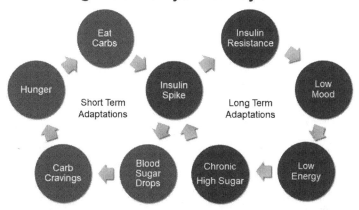

http://blog.nodiabetes.in/insulin-resistance-causes-type-2-diabetespart-2/

Some say the solution is to eat whole grains, assuming their slower release of sugars will help protect us. But the truth is that all carbohydrates are converted in the body to simple sugar. It doesn't matter if the carbohydrates come from whole grains or complex carbohydrates or a chocolate cake. The body breaks it all down, and the result is the same.

With a ceaseless intake of sugar, we put our bodies in a constant crisis mode, pumping out more and more insulin. Over time, the tissues that store glucose becomes insulin resistant, requiring higher amounts of insulin to do the same job. The cells in the pancreas that make insulin begin to fail, exhausted by the constant effort, and blood sugar remains high. We become metabolically damaged. When this gets diagnosed with an actual disease, it's called type 2 diabetes.

Note: Slide Source http://blog.nodiabetes.in/insulin-resistance-causes-type-2-diabetespart-2

Consequences of High Insulin

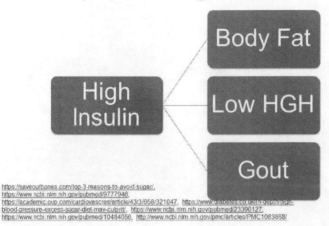

Sustained high insulin levels have other consequences. Insulin inhibits the breakdown of fat cells and stimulates the creation of body fat. Insulin tells the body to stop burning its fat stores and instead, absorb some of the fatty acids and glucose in the blood and turn them into more body fat. It's like a gear stick stuck in reverse. Our bodies can't burn stored fat unless our insulin levels are low.

High insulin also affects our muscles directly. To grow muscle, our bodies make another hormone called HGH -- the human growth hormone. But HGH and insulin are antagonists. High insulin suppresses HGH. There's a saying that when you get stronger, you are turning fat into muscle. High insulin turns our muscle into fat.

Gout, a very painful type of inflammatory arthritis, is caused by too much uric acid in the blood. But the high uric acid level itself is caused by a combination of sugar and insulin. Consuming fructose, a type of sugar sharply increases levels of uric acid in the body. High insulin levels, triggered by high sugar, increase uric acid levels further by decreasing the excretion of uric acid by the kidneys.

Note: Slide Sources: saveourbones.com/top-3-reasons-to-avoid-sugar/, www.ncbi.nlm.nih.gov/pubmed/9777946, academic.oup.com/ cardiovascres/ article/43/3/658/321047, diabetes.co.uk/in-depth/high-blood-pressure-excess-sugar-diet-may-culprit/, ncbi.nlm.nih.gov/pubmed/23390127, ncbi.nlm.nih.gov/ pubmed/10484056, ncbi.nlm.nih.gov/pmc/articles/PMC1083868/

Consequences of High Sugar

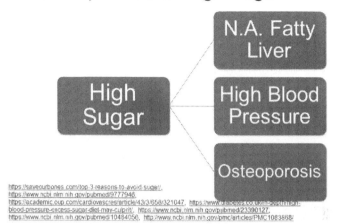

High intake of fructose, a type of sugar, is what causes non-alcoholic fatty liver.

High sugar intake causes high blood pressure. Insulin resistance blocks the storage of magnesium, keeping blood vessels from relaxing and driving up blood pressure. Fructose sugar, specifically, elevates uric acid, which drives up blood pressure by inhibiting the nitric oxide (NO) in blood vessels. This constricts the blood vessels and promotes inflammation and oxidative stress. By the way, that Nitric Oxide issue? That's the primary cause of erectile dysfunction.

Osteoporosis: high sugar intake generates Advanced Glycation End products - proteins that have been bonded to sugar molecules. AGEs cause widespread destruction, weakening the collagen that gives our bones a strong foundation. And sugar robs our bones of the minerals that keep them strong: calcium, magnesium, and copper. And that calcium? It goes into your blood vessels, hardening your arteries with atherosclerosis.

Note: Slide Sources: saveourbones.com/top-3-reasons-to-avoid-sugar/, www.ncbi.nlm.nih.gov/pubmed/9777946, academic.oup.com/ cardiovascres/ article/43/3/658/321047, diabetes.co.uk/in-depth/high-blood-pressure-excess-sugar-diet-may-culprit/, ncbi.nlm.nih.gov/pubmed/23390127, ncbi.nlm.nih.gov/ pubmed/10484056, ncbi.nlm.nih.gov/pmc/articles/PMC1083868/

How Sick Are We?

150m	**175m**	**92m**
Diabetes or Pre-Diabetes	Overweight or Obese	Cardiovascular Disease

86m	**44m**
High Blood Pressure	Osteoporosis or Low Bone Mass

Statistics from: https://www.cdc.gov/diabetes/pdfs/data/statistics/national-diabetes-statistics-report.pdf,https://www.iofbonehealth.org/facts-statistics, https://www.cdc.gov/nchs/fastats/obesity-overweight.htm, https://healthmetrics.heart.org/wp-content/uploads/2017/06/Heart-Disease-and-Stroke-Statistics-2017-ucm_491265.pdf

When we look back at those disease numbers now, what we see is that the majority of Americans have been damaged by a high carbohydrate diet. From processed foods high in sugar and refined grains. Young and old, fat and thin. The damage is nearly universal.

So what can we do about it? Can we do anything to stop the damage? Is there any chance it can be reversed?

Yes. By understanding how food affects our bodies and by making the right choices. By working with our biochemistry instead of against it.

Note: Slide Statistics from: https://www.cdc.gov/diabetes/pdfs/data/statistics/national-diabetes-statistics-report.pdf,https://www.iofbonehealth.org/facts-statistics, https://www.cdc.gov/nchs/fastats/obesity-overweight.htm, https://healthmetrics.heart.org/wp-content/uploads/2017/06/Heart-Disease-and-Stroke-Statistics-2017-ucm_491265.pdf

Insulin and Macronutrients

Glucose/Insulin Reaction to Macronutrients

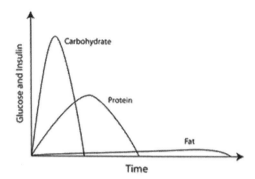

We've seen how high-carbohydrate intake leads to high insulin, and how both are destructive over the long term. But we still need to get our calories from somewhere, and there are only three macronutrients available to the human body.

This chart shows the insulin responses of carbohydrates, protein, and fat. Sugar causes the highest response, so we need to keep carbohydrates to a minimum. But protein also creates a moderate response, so we don't want to go overboard on protein either. The only macronutrient that causes minimal insulin response is fat.

What about just eating less of everything? This only works for a short time because calorie restriction diets are unsustainable. In the end, we get too hungry to maintain them. But worse than that, when we starve ourselves while still eating a high carb diet, our bodies will self-cannibalize, breaking down muscle to reduce energy needs, surviving on the calories from our body protein instead of the fact that we should be burning. And when we resume our normal eating patterns, our metabolisms remain permanently lowered, causing us to gain back everything we've lost and more. A dieting pattern that is familiar to many of us.

The Low-Carb Diet

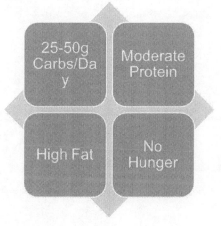

That at last brings us to the low-carb diet. On a low-carb diet, our bodies switch our primary fuel source from sugar to fat. With low insulin, our bodies are finally able to access the energy in our fat stores.

A low-carb diet is based on meat, poultry, seafood, eggs, nuts, non-starchy vegetables, low-sugar fruits, and healthy fats. It is a very low carbohydrate, moderate protein, and high fat. A low-carb diet is NOT a calorie-restricting starvation diet. It should not leave you hungry between meals. It is easily sustainable over the long term -- in fact, for a lifetime. It's how our hunter-gatherer ancestors ate and thrived before the invention of agriculture and all the diseases that came with it.

Without high sugar and high insulin, Advanced Glycation End products decrease; triglycerides decrease; type-B LDL is replaced by type-A LDL, and good HDL cholesterol levels increase. All the markers of heart disease improve dramatically.

Before and After

Before (on Standard American Diet, with statins)
- Cholesterol 229
- Triglycerides 156
- HDL 39
- LDL 159.8

After (on Ketogenic Diet)
- Cholesterol: 140
- Triglycerides: 104
- HDL: 44
- LDL: 77

Here is an example from my father, who suffered a heart attack at age 50. He had triple bypass surgery, then spent 20 years on low-fat diets that did nothing to improve his lipid panel. And now, after less than a year on low-carb, he has gone from this to this. His cholesterol alone went from 229 to 140. Thanks to a low-carb diet, he is now able to transition off of statins and blood pressure medication. By medical definition, he is "cured" -- as long as he doesn't go back to eating carbohydrates.

What Fats Are Healthy?

The modern low-carb diet focuses on maximum nutrition as well as minimum insulin response. One key aspect is dietary fat.

Again, we must get our calories from somewhere. A high-protein diet would be as unsustainable as a high-carbohydrate diet. What's left for us to eat is fat. Some of that will come from our stored body fat, but the rest must come from our diet. We must also eat dietary fat so that our livers will be stimulated to generate the necessary enzymes for fat burning.

Refined Vegetable Oils

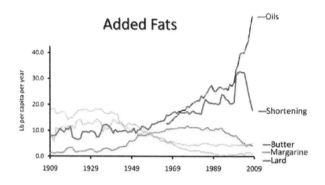

Source: Dr. Stephan Guyenet. The American Diet. 2012.

In the era of low-fat diets, saturated fats have been demonized. For decades, we have been directed to use polyunsaturated vegetable oils like canola oil, soybean oil, corn oil, and margarine. But this advice was made under the assumption that saturated fat caused heart disease, and that hypothesis has been proven wrong. Dietary fats do not cause heart disease. Saturated fats do not cause heart disease.

But what is the safest kind of fat to eat?

The primary determining quality of the worth of dietary fat is its stability: whether or not it is prone to oxidation. We all know oxidation is a bad thing -- that's why there's so much interest in antioxidants -- but we're also familiar with it by another word: rancid. And some fats go rancid very quickly.

Note: Slide source: EDxHarvardLaw - Stephan **Guyenet** - The **American Diet**. TEDx Talks 2012

Saturated vs Unsaturated

```
        O  H  H  H
        ||  |  |  |
   H-O-C-C-C-C-H
        |  |  |
        H  H  H
```
Butyric Acid-Saturated Fatty Acid

```
      O  H  H  H  H  H  H  H  ↓  H  H  H  H  H  H  H  H
      ||  |  |  |  |  |  |  |     |  |  |  |  |  |  |  |
 H-O-C-C-C-C-C-C-C- C-C=C-C-C-C-C-C-C-C-C-H
      |  |  |  |  |  |  |  |  |  |  |  |  |  |  |  |  |
      H  H  H  H  H  H  H  H  H  H  H  H  H  H  H  H
```
Oleic Acid- Monounsaturated Fatty Acid

```
      O  H  H  H  H  ↓     H  ↓  H  H  H  H  H  H  H  H
      ||  |  |  |  |  |        |     |  |  |  |  |  |  |  |
 H-O-C-C-C-C-C-C=C- C-C=C-C-C-C-C-C-C-C-C-H
      |  |  |  |  |  |     |  |  |  |  |  |  |  |  |  |  |
      H  H  H  H  H  H  H  H  H  H  H  H  H  H  H  H
```
Linoleic Acid- Polyunsaturated Fatty Acid

There are three types of fat: saturated, monounsaturated, and polyunsaturated. These names tell us a lot about the nature of each kind of fat. Saturated fat is a type of fat in which the fatty acid chains have all or predominantly single bonds. It is saturated with hydrogen bonds. In unsaturated fats, the more double bonds present, the more vulnerable the fatty acids are to oxidation and rancidity. Polyunsaturated fatty acids are delicate and easily oxidized by light, air, and heat. Saturated fatty acids (SFAs) and monounsaturated fatty acids (MUFAs) are less susceptible to being oxidized and can stand up to more cooking heat than PUFAs can.

Why does rancidity matter? When an unsaturated fat oxidizes, through exposure to light and heat from cooking, those double bonds cause it to break down into unstable molecules that are disruptive in the body. These damaged fats are highly oxidative; they are 'unsaturated' because they lack an at least one oxygen molecule. They obtain this oxygen molecule by inducing reactions in our bodies that produce oxygen: this is oxidization. Rancid fats steal oxygen molecules from your cells. They disrupt metabolic processes, damage cells, and cause inflammation. Oxidization leaves tiny wounds in your arterial walls, wounds which can fill up with calcium molecules that are free-floating in your blood because of sugar. Oxidation-damaged arteries clogged with calcium: this is atherosclerosis.

Fatty Acid Compositions

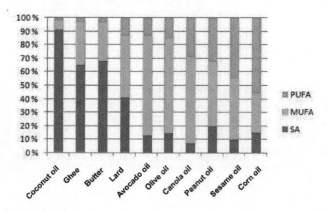

For this reason, the low-carb diet avoids unstable polyunsaturated fats, especially polyunsaturated vegetable oils, which are created with an industrial process that is so intense that those fats are rancid before they are even put into a bottle.

All fats and oils contain each of the three types of fatty acid, but the quantities of each are key. Coconut oil is the most stable at over 90% saturated fat. Ghee, butter, and animal fats like lard are also excellent, with minimal polyunsaturated fat. Primarily monounsaturated fats like avocado oil are also fairly safe for cooking. But vegetable oils such as corn and canola are 30% polyunsaturated fat or higher. The smoke point is also important. This is the temperature at which an oil will start to burn, oxidizing and generating smoke. Olive oil, for example, while relatively low in polyunsaturated fats, is easily damaged by heat and should not be used for cooking, though it is safe for uses such as salad dressing.

Mitochondria and Fat

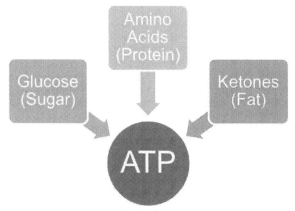

https://www.ncbi.nlm.nih.gov/pmc/articles/PMC2129159/

So, beyond insulin and sugar, how do our bodies change on a low-carb, high-fat diet? Let's start with our cells. Almost every cell in our bodies contains mitochondria. This is the part of our cells that convert the sugar, fat, and protein in our food and bodies into adenosine triphosphate, or ATP. We need a lot of ATP to survive, around 10 million molecules of ATP per second for every cell.

Our mitochondria can use any of the macronutrients as fuel, but not all fuels are the same. Protein and sugar offer only four calories of energy per gram, while fat offers nine calories per gram. While sugar is the fastest to burn, it is also the messiest, producing reactive oxygen and free radicals that cause damage to our cells. Protein can be used as a fuel source, but it is usually needed elsewhere in the body for the growth and repair of tissues. Energy-dense fat produces the least oxidative stress and the most ATP.

When fat powers our mitochondria, they not only work better, but they multiply. A low-carb, high-fat diet stimulates the creation of new mitochondria throughout the body and the brain. Now our cells have more energy available to them, and our mitochondria don't have to work as hard to provide it. This makes our cells more efficient.

Note: Slide source https://www.ncbi.nlm.nih.gov/pmc/articles/PMC2129159/

Body and Brain Benefits

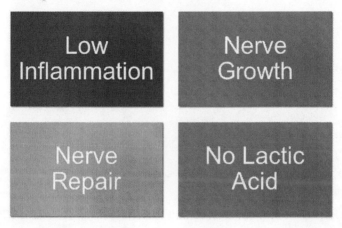

Let's move up to a higher level. Less oxidative stress means a decrease in inflammation throughout the body and brain. This prevents damage to the brain cells that would otherwise occur on a high-carbohydrate diet. The change in diet triggers an increase in brain-derived neurotrophic factor and nerve growth factor. These stimulate the growth and repair of nerves in both the brain and central nervous system, improving learning, memory, and higher thinking.

Our muscles work better with fat, too. We're all familiar with the burn of lactic acid from exercises. Lactic acid is a byproduct of the conversion of sugar into ATP. But when fat fuels our cells, lactic acid is not produced. This allows us to exercise longer, without fighting muscle burn.

Therapeutic Uses

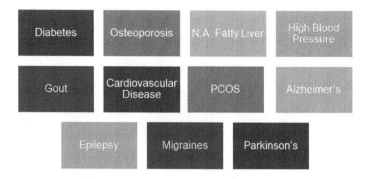

Low-carb, high-fat diets can be used therapeutically for many diseases. We've covered several already: diabetes, osteoporosis, non-alcoholic fatty liver, high blood pressure, gout, and cardiovascular disease. It also works wonders for Poly-Cystic Ovarian Syndrome or PCOS. PCOS is another disease of civilization, sometimes called a metabolic, reproductive disorder. Studies have shown significant improvements in weight, testosterone levels, hormone levels, and fasting insulin, potentially restoring fertility and reducing the risk of pregnancy-related complications like gestational diabetes, pre-eclampsia, and overweight babies.

Recent research has shown that blood sugar glucose and Alzheimer's disease are linked. Some researchers have even referred to Alzheimer's as "type 3 diabetes" because it may be a late-stage of type 2 diabetes. As blood sugar levels and insulin resistance increase so does the progression of Alzheimer's disease. In studies, minimizing insulin and carbohydrates improves cognitive performance and behavioral issues of those with the disease.

Low-carb has been a powerful treatment for epilepsy for decades, improving or clearing seizures in about 50% of patients, both children, and adults. Similar benefits have been seen in studies for migraine sufferers, in some cases achieving 90% clearance. And patients with Parkinson's Disease, a nervous system disorder characterized by low levels of the signaling molecule dopamine, have shown improved motor function.

How To Get Started

The science is clear. The standard American diet, rich in refined starches, sugars, and polyunsaturated fats, has done tremendous damage to our health. Our government and food industries made the wrong choice back in the 20th century, and we are all paying the price.

The good news is that it's not too late for us to reclaim our health, to prevent and even reverse terrible health problems. If we remove the sugar and other carbohydrates from our diets and replace them with healthy fats and moderate proteins, we can help our bodies heal and thrive. We only must make the right choice.

What I'm handing out now is an introductory guide to a low-carb, high-fat diet. It contains tips on how to change from burning sugar to fat, what foods to eat in grocery stores and restaurants, a guide to cooking fats, and a list of the dozens of names for sugar found in 74% of supermarket products.

APPENDIX B BACKGROUND LINKS

In retirement, the impact of not being physically fit impacts strongly what paths can be chosen. If you have trouble walking, it makes it very difficult to go on a nature hike.

There is a significant amount of research going into the effects of food on health. Two-thirds of Americans are morbidly obese, and the health and financial impacts are immense. These links below bring you to research on how food has been changed to contain toxic levels of carbohydrates and sugars to increase your consumption and purchases. The food industry, like the tobacco industry, appears to have known this for some time and has used its money and resources to mask the truth.

We concentrate on added sugar and carbohydrates as two items in your diet that result in excessive weight, anxiety, and suppression of ordinary body control.

Added Sugar

- Sugar usage:
  http://www.nhs.uk/Livewell/Goodfood/Pages/sugars.aspx

- Dr. Lustig research on fructose poisoning
  - Sugar the Bitter Truth - https://www.youtube.com/watch?v=dBnniu a6-oM
  - **Add other video links here**
- Three reasons to avoid sugar - https://saveourbones.com/top-3-reasons-to-avoid-sugar/

Carbohydrates

- Low fat vs. low carbohydrates diets - https://www.ncbi.nlm.nih.gov/pubmed/12640371
- Ted Talk to remove carbs to reverse diabetes - https://www.youtube.com/watch?v=da1vvigy5tQ
- Low-Carbohydrate Diet Superior to Antipsychotic Medications https://www.psychologytoday.com/blog/diagnosis-diet/201709/low-carbohydrate-diet-superior-antipsychotic-medications
- Nash Diet - http://www.medicinenet.com/fatty_liver/page2.htm
- Food as a sedative - https://www.nbcnews.com/better/diet-fitness/what-eat-if-you-want-go-sleep-faster-n769386
- Lower triglycerides
  - https://www.nemechekconsultativemedicine.com/blog/lower-your-triglycerides-without-taking-medication/
- Netflix series on "Food." Goes into why the bread we buy is not bread anymore
- Canadian revising food plan in support of low carbohydrate, high-fat diets -

- https://www.treehugger.com/health/canadian-physicians-say-its-time-low-carb-high-fat-food-guide.html
- https://mail.google.com/mail/u/0/#inbox/1619 58c56d7dc4f2

Heart Disease

- Ketosis and heart attacks
  - A study showing significant improvement - https://www.ncbi.nlm.nih.gov/pmc/articles/PMC2716748/
  - Case study measuring plaque reduction - https://www.docmuscles.com/vascular-plaque-reduction-with-ketogenic-diet-a-case-study/
  - Insulin, not fat causes clogged arteries - https://www.youtube.com/watch?v=HmJSw0x3Rl0
  - Other illnesses affected by Ketosis diet.
    - Illnesses that can be affected by ketosis diet - https://www.healthline.com/nutrition/15-conditions-benefit-ketogenic-diet#section1
    - More rigorous review of another disease in NIH site - https://www.ncbi.nlm.nih.gov/pmc/articles/PMC2898565/
  - Eating saturated fat does not clog arteries - http://www.clareharding.com/if-saturated-fat-does-not-clog-up-arteries-what-does-cholesterol-5/
  - List of doctors supporting low carb eating

program - http://lowcarbdoctors.blogspot.com/

- Scientific American article on a diet results not published
  - https://www.scientificamerican.com/article/records-found-in-dusty-basement-undermine-decades-of-dietary-advice/?wt.mc=SA_Facebook-Share

Skin Conditions
- Muscle and skin tone - use of collagen to improve muscle and skin tone
  - http://www.perfect-supplements.com/health-benefits-of-collagen/
  - https://www.medicalnewstoday.com/articles/262881.php

Diet effects heath
- Six studies that link food and health that show that foods labeled as "bad" may be beneficial. - https://www.marksdailyapple.com/6-older-studies-that-got-no-love-but-should-have/

APPENDIX C WHY AMA AND ADA RECOMMENDATIONS ARE IN QUESTION

- Associations
    - o AMA – American Medical Associations
    - o ADA – American Diabetes Association
    - o AHA – American Heart Association

- NYTimes op editorial detailing studies showing the AMA diet is wrong: Contains extensive links to reviews and official government reports - https://www.nytimes.com/2015/02/21/opinion/when-the-government-tells-you-what-to-eat.html
- American Heart Association uses bad science to support dietary recommendations. - https://www.thedailybeast.com/the-heart-associations-junk-science-diet
- Low-fat diets history and why they are wrong - https://academic.oup.com/jhmas/article/63/2/139/772615

.

APPENDIX D REFERENCES

---

[i] Loss of social environment associated with working is a killer among retires: https: //www.fool.com/slideshow/silent-killer-among-american-retirees/?slide=3

[ii] Divorce rates over the last 10 years for 55 + are up 110% http://www.pewresearch.org/fact-tank/2017/03/09/led-by-baby-boomers-divorce-rates-climb-for-americas-50-population/

[iii] Jim real life systems trainer at a large corporation

[iv] References about the men and women accepting death. https://www.ncbi.nlm.nih.gov/pmc/articles/PMC4828197/

[v] Covey, Stephen R. *The 7 Habits of Highly Effective People: Restoring the Character Ethic.* [Rev. ed.]. New York: Free Press, 2004.

[vi] Retires returning to work in Japan- https://www.npr.org/sections/parallels/2016/08/25/490687317/for-some-older-adults-in-japan-a-chance-to-stay-in-the-workforce money.usnews.com/money/retirement/articles/2014/01/21/7-reasons-not-to-move-in-retirement

[vii] Survey of decision making. - http://www.pewsocialtrends.org/2008/09/25/women-call-the-shots-at-home-public-mixed-on-gender-roles-in-jobs/

[viii] Nielsen survey on percentages by area men vs women vs joint purchasing control. – http://www.nielsen.com/us/en/insights/news/2013/u-s--women-control-the-purse-strings.html

[ix] Seniors in Japanese labor force:
http://www.nber.org/chapters/c14047.pdf

[x] How the Amish handle retirement:
http://www.amishquilter.com/retirement-in-the-amish-community/

[xi] Networking site to find others with similar interest:
https://www.meetup.com/

[xii] Divorce rates over the last 10 years for 55 + are up 110%
http://www.pewresearch.org/fact-tank/2017/03/09/led-by-baby-boomers-divorce-rates-climb-for-americas-50-population/

[xiii] Active listening:
https://en.wikipedia.org/wiki/Active_listening

[xiv] Men are from Mars, Women are form Venus:
https://en.wikipedia.org/wiki/Men_Are_from_Mars,_Women_Are_from_Venus

[xv] Women like BFF over Husband –
https://www.msn.com/en-us/video/viral/a-lot-of-women-prefer-their-bff-over-their-husband/vp-AAvyPsM

[xvi] Article on how long it takes to make a friend. -
https://www.cnn.com/2018/04/23/health/acquaintance-friend-partner/index.html

[xvii] MacGuffin:
https://en.wikipedia.org/wiki/MacGuffin

[xviii] Mayo Clinic on benefits of walking, stepping -
https://www.mayoclinic.org/healthy-lifestyle/fitness/in-depth/walking/art-20046261

[xix] How your body changes on the inside as you age, e.g. wear out:
https://orthoinfo.aaos.org/en/staying-healthy/effects-of-aging/

[xx] How your feet change with age:
https://health.clevelandclinic.org/2016/04/shoes-getting-tight-feet-change-size-time/

[xxi] How many steps per day is recommended for an adult:
https://www.ncbi.nlm.nih.gov/pmc/articles/PMC3169444/

xxii Effective half-life antibiotics reference: -
https://en.wikibooks.org/wiki/What_You_Should_Know_About_Medicines/Half_life,_or_how_often_to_take_it

xxiii How many attempts to break a habit:
https://jamesclear.com/new-habit

xxiv Loop Counter:
https://www.amazon.com/SportCount-LapCounter/dp/B0016J9NE8/ref=sr_1_19_sspa?ie=UTF8&qid=1516321000&sr=8-19-spons&keywords=ring+counter&psc=1

xxv Use of muscle groups when walking:
https://www.ncbi.nlm.nih.gov/pmc/articles/PMC3870652/

xxvi Resistance training is Medicine:
https://www.ncbi.nlm.nih.gov/pubmed/22777332

xxvii Sugar consumption level recommended in England:
https://www.nhs.uk/news/food-and-diet/sugar-intake-should-be-drastically-reduced-says-report/

xxviii Lustig video on YouTube:
https://www.youtube.com/watch?v=dBnniua6-oM

Lustig books on Amazon:
https://www.amazon.com/Fat-Chance-Beating-Against-Processed/dp/0142180432/ref=sr_1_1?ie=UTF8&qid=1526386535&sr=8-1&keywords=lustig+sugar

xxix Cocoa replace cocaine with sugar reference:
https://en.wikipedia.org/wiki/Coca-Cola#19th-century_historical_origins

xxx Lack of nutrition in Wonder Bread:
http://thenakedlabel.com/blog/2012/04/23/wonder-bread-not-wonderful-for-your-health/

xxxi Windrower symptoms: https://www.ncbi.nlm.nih.gov/pubmed/7086634

xxxii Reference hormones for appetite control:
https://www.ncbi.nlm.nih.gov/pubmed/17212793
https://www.ncbi.nlm.nih.gov/pmc/articles/PMC2777281/
https://www.ncbi.nlm.nih.gov/pubmedhealth/PMH0072573/

xxxiii Sugar is in 74% of all processed foods:
http://sugarscience.ucsf.edu/hidden-in-plain-sight/#.WmyFKWinFhE

xxxiv Book Sugar Blues by William Duffy:
https://en.wikipedia.org/wiki/Sugar_Blues

xxxv Sugar the Bitter Truth Video by Dr. Lustig:
https://www.youtube.com/watch?v=T8G8tLsl_A4

xxxvi Effect of sugar and carbohyrates on your hormonal system:
https://www.marksdailyapple.com/what-happens-to-your-body-when-you-carb-binge/

NIH Published paper:
https://www.ncbi.nlm.nih.gov/pmc/articles/PMC4644820/

xxxvii Carbohydrate toxicity -
https://www.ncbi.nlm.nih.gov/pmc/articles/PMC4224210/

xxxviii https://breaknutrition.com/keto-flu/
xxxix Carbohydrate level in sub sandwich -
https://www.eatthismuch.com/food/view/submarine-sandwich,5044/

xl MyFitnessPal Application:
http://www.myfitnesspal.com/food/calories/generic-sub-sandwich-bread-149826164

xli Fat as a fuel source NIH article - Fats as fuel source NIH
https://www.ncbi.nlm.nih.gov/pubmed/20353493
https://www.ncbi.nlm.nih.gov/pubmed/25275931

xlii Symptoms of drug addiction -
https://www.drugabuse.gov/publications/principles-drug-addiction-treatment-research-based-guide-third-edition/frequently-asked-questions/why-do-drug-addicted-persons-keep-using

xliii Drug addiction relapse:
https://drugabuse.com/library/drug-relapse/

xliv Symptoms of relapse:
https://drugabuse.com/library/drug-relapse/

xlv Product description of MyFitnessPal-
https://www.pcmag.com/article2/0,2817,2393270,00.asp

xlvi HGH availability –
https://www.ncbi.nlm.nih.gov/pubmed/17212793

xlvii Over eating hormonal -
https://www.ncbi.nlm.nih.gov/pubmed/17212793

xlviii Added sugar in processed foods:
https://www.nytimes.com/2016/05/22/upshot/it-isnt-easy-to-figure-out-which-foods-contain-sugar.html

xlix Reduced consumption when on Ketosis like eating
https://www.ncbi.nlm.nih.gov/pubmed/25402637

Made in the USA
Columbia, SC
18 June 2024

37261874R00121